TSUKEMONO
Japanese Pickled Vegetables

TSUKEMONO
Japanese Pickled Vegetables

Kay Shimizu

Shufunotomo Co., Ltd.

First printing, 1993

© Copyright in Japan 1993 by Kay Shimizu and
    Shufunotomo Co., Ltd.
Illustrations by Office 21
Collages by Tokue Terada
Photographs by Shufunotomo Co., Ltd.

Recipes by
Toshio Ogawa, Keiko Hanagata, Ikuko Hisamatsu,
Reiko Sakai, Fumiko Makita, Akiko Murakami,
Fumiko Kimura, Hatsu Hirano, Hiroko Fukami,
Sumiko Fujita, Tokiko Suzuki, Kiyoko Endo,
Toyoko Ishii and Kay Shimizu

Published by Shufunotomo Co., Ltd.
2-9, Kanda Surugadai, Chiyoda-ku, Tokyo, 101 Japan

ISBN: 4-07-975010-2
Printed in Japan

Dedication

I acknowledge with special thanks those persons who shared their assistance, advice and experience in this production.

Shunichi Kamiya and Michiko Kinoshita of Shufunotomo Co., translator Keiko Ito, Americans Nobue Malone, Sumi Shimoda and Tats Tanaka for their *tsukemono* expertise.

PREFACE

"Something soaked or marinated" would be the literal translation for the traditional Japanese *tsukemono*. It is not truly a pickle, however, in the Western concept. Some are more delicate and others have a refreshingly bold taste. Some are made instantly and others take months or years.

Pickling is a manner of conserving and capturing the fresh vitamin enriched, natural pristine flavors of diverse vegetables and fruits. *Tsukemono* techniques are many and varied, depending upon geographic regions and secret family recipes. Then there is *kajitsu-shu*, a fruit liqueur, so very delicate, light and embodying the essence of the fresh fruit. A selection of Pacific Rim pickles is also included.

I have edited recipes from Japanese experts and also included my Americanized versions adapted to the Western palate. This book will tempt the fanatics at cooking, at eating or at collecting cookbooks. *Tsukemono* served traditionally at meal's end with rice and green tea clears the mouth and aids digestion. Even if you eat nothing else, rice, *tsukemono* and tea can be most satisfying. There is no equivalent in the Western menu for this combination, which yields such comfort and pleasure all in one! Beware, you can become addicted.

Consume in watchful moderation. Savor a bite as an appetizer or even as snack food for a taste adventure to humdrum meals. Avoid excessive use of salt for healthy living, but a little extra salt occasionally will allow you to enjoy a full repertoire of flavor sensations. *Tsukemono*, with its interesting, creative flavors, is outrageously good. Increasingly, more Japanese food shops in Western cities display *tsukemono* in a multitude of varieties. Some even offer tastings. Such a myriad of mystifying choices and smells! The savory goodness of *tsukemono*, *kajitsu-shu* and Pacific Rim pickles can be enjoyed with all kinds of international meals, although *tsukemono* is uniquely Japanese. Enjoy!

Kay Shimizu
Saratoga, CA

CONTENTS

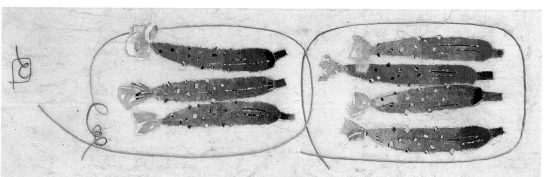

HISTORY OF *TSUKEMONO*

The origins of *tsukemono* are vague. It is believed, however, that once the collection of sea water was discovered, pickling of vegetables began. In ancient times, pickling and drying were the only methods of preserving food for future use. The world's two oldest kinds of pickles are sauerkraut from Europe and *zha cai* from China.

Tsukemono was no doubt introduced into Japan from China, but Japan subsequently developed its own characteristic style based on local tastes and produce. In Japan, respect for vegetables and salt became an integral part of the Shinto religion. It was believed that vegetables and salt were the Gods' precious gifts to the people, necessary for general good health.

One theory about the origins of *tsukemono* is that shrine offerings included vegetables and salt. Quantities were heaped on the altar, and as days passed, fermentation occurred. The fragrant taste and aroma that resulted were found to be pleasurable. *Tsukemono* in ancient Japan was called *konomono* or *ko-ko*, which translates as "fragrant things."

The earliest evidence of *tsukemono* in Japan was found in a document called "Zomotsu Osamecho," discovered at Nara's Todaiji Temple. This document was written over 1,000 years ago, during the reign of Emperor Keiko in the 4th century A.D.

Tsukemono that existed during the Edo Period (1603–1867) are well documented. From writings of the time, we know that such pickles as *bettara-zuke, fukujin-zuke, omi-zuke,* and *takuan* existed then.

Festivals celebrating *tsukemono* are held throughout Japan. This illustrates the respect and appreciation that traditional Japanese have for pickled vegetables. Each locality has developed its own style of *tsukemono*, and these are sold in specially designed packaging to be purchased as gifts. They are a favorite type of souvenir for travelers. Is there any other country in the world whose people revere pickles as much as the Japanese?

NUTRITIONAL VALUE OF *TSUKEMONO*

DIETARY FIBER

Dietary fiber is missing in many people's diets, resulting in modern diseases. This dietary fiber is the general name of indigestible ingredients of food which are not absorbed in the body and are discharged as excrement. Fiber is vital to good health. Without fiber one can get constipation resulting in gastroenteric disorders, cancer of the large intestines, as well as diabetes.

In addition, dietary fiber activates lactobacillus bifidus, a useful bacterium within the intestines. It resolves nitrosamine, a carcinogen, restrains harmful bacteria and does other important actions.

Vegetables, fruit and seaweed have an abundance of these fibers, but with few calories or little protein. Vegetable pickles (*tsukemono*) contain more fiber than fresh vegetables, since water is removed in the pickling process. Some examples of vegetable dietary fiber are as follows:

	100 g serving
Chinese *nappa* cabbage (fresh)	0.84 mg
Chinese *nappa* cabbage (salted)	3.4 mg
Daikon (fresh)	0.89 mg
Daikon tsukemono (*Takuan*)	2.9 mg

THE ACID EFFECT OF PICKLES

Organic acids such as malic acid or acetic acid have significant effects in the body. When we eat grain or meat they are digested and absorbed in the body, then burned to supply the energy needed for our activities. *Tsukemono* contains acid so it facilitates this burning action, which assists the body's recovery from fatigue or illness and prevents accumulation of fats, resulting in a slimmer body. All pickles contain acids to a greater or lesser degree. Vinegared vegetables and *umeboshi* are *tsukemono* flavored mainly by acids. To consume more acids, one can mix vegetables with apple, which contains an abundance of maltic or citric acid.

VITAMIN CONTENT

Many vegetables have excellent natural medicinal effects and are also sources of vitamins. Vegetables of orange or deep green colors are rich sources of vitamin A and carotene, such as carrots, green peppers and *shiso*. Vitamin C is found in fresh vegetables, fruits, and seaweed, but not contained in fish, meat, poultry or grain.

Vitamin C in vegetables is destroyed if they are pickled too long. Therefore use vegetables containing vitamin C for your instant type pickling methods.

Nuka-zuke is rich in vitamin B_1 and B_2, containing several times as much vitamin B as fresh vegetables. In the *nuka-zuke* pickling process, water-soluble vitamin B contained in *nuka* soaks into the vegetables. No food contains more vitamin B than *nuka*-pickled *tsukemono*.

Examples of Vitamin B_1 and B_2

	100 g serving	
	Vit. B_1	Vit. B_2
Turnip tops (fresh)	0.07 mg	0.15 mg
Turnip tops (*nuka zuke*)	0.27 mg	0.21 mg
Daikon root (fresh)	0.03 mg	0.02 mg
Daikon (*nuka-zuke*)	0.36 mg	0.04 mg

Examples of Vitamin C

	100 g serving
Turnip tops (fresh)	43 mg
Turnip tops (*nuka-zuke*)	75 mg
Chinese *nappa* cabbage (fresh)	29 mg
Chinese *nappa* cabbage (salted)	22 mg

CALCIUM CONTENT

Calcium and other minerals build strong bones, teeth and help in the general growth of bodies. Vegetables contain calcium, potassium, iron, etc., and pickling retains them well. Eating *tsukemono* helps your body to take in sufficient minerals.

Examples of calcium

	100 g serving
Chinese *nappa* cabbage (fresh)	35 mg
Chinese *nappa* cabbage (salted)	50 mg
Daikon (fresh)	30 mg
Daikon tsukemono (Takuan)	55 mg

(All the above examples are from the Japanese government *Table of Standard Constituent Elements of Japanese Foods*, the fourth revision, Science and Technology Agency, 1991.)

ENZYMES

Pickles help digestion by aiding the secretion of saliva and gastric juices, which contribute to the body's metabolic rhythm. The enzymes in pickles facilitate secretion of digestive juices.

Enzymes are destroyed by heat. Since *tsukemono* is not heat-treated, enzymes remain active and the absorption in the stomach and intestines is excellent. *Tsukemono* is a coordinator of gastro-intestinal action and acts as a sterilizer. It destroys pathogenic bacteria and helps propagation of useful bacteria like lactobacillus bifidus. *Umeboshi* has been recommended as a preventive for infectious diseases.

When we consume food, it reaches the stomach and gastric juices are secreted. The hydrochloric acid contained in the juice keeps the food in weak acidity, activates the digestive enzyme action and prevents abnormal fermentation of food.

Pickles contain certain kinds of organic acids which can help to keep the weak acidity balance within the stomach and intestines and stimulate the action of the gastro-intestinal wall.

HEALTHY *TSUKEMONO*

Nutrition is not lost by making vegetables into *tsukemono*. Vegetables often have to be cooked to remove harsh flavors, however, with pickling of vegetables Japanese-style the bitterness can be removed. As an example, note that eggplant after pickling firms up and the water is drawn out. The result is a vegetable that is "easy to eat."

Originally *tsukemono* was salted heavily to preserve the vegetable for a long time, but today we do not need to store for such long periods. Modern shipping and distribution make fresh produce available all year round. And, we have our faithful refrigerators.

For health reasons we should begin to use less salt in our foods. The ideal is to salt as lightly as possible and serve the *tsukemono* before it is excessively seasoned. Eat small servings to reduce salt intake.

For a salt substitute when making *tsukemono*, one can use alcohol or vinegar. In the pickling process, water is removed with the help of the high osmotic pressure of salt. This breaks down the cells of the vegetable and prevents spoilage. Longer preservation can be achieved by replacing salt with white liquor in a 1–3 ratio in making *shio-zuke, nuka-zuke, shoyu-zuke* or other *tsukemono*.

Acid, the main ingredient of vinegar, kills almost all putrefactive bacteria when vinegar is added to food in an amount equal to 2% of the food's weight. So you can replace salt with vinegar. Add a little vinegar in making overnight *tsukemono*. Vinegar is good for your health and some types of sour pickles go especially well with meat and oily dishes. At the same time, when serving Chinese dishes be sure to grate some *daikon* since its diastase aids digestion. You may have noticed that *tempura* always has a tiny mound of *daikon* served on the side.

Pickles are sometimes called "*oshinko*," which literally means new aromas. Best served in small portions. In Japan, they are usually served at the end of a meal, together with rice and tea.

The unique flavors of *tsukemono* are the result of fermentation. Adding spices or herbs such as ginger, *shiso, myoga,* red chili pepper, garlic or *sansho* enhances the delicate pickle flavors. A strongly flavored pickle stimulates the appetite.

EQUIPMENT FOR *TSUKEMONO* MAKING

PICKLING CONTAINERS
* Choose a handy size for your family's needs. For small quantities to be kept in refrigerator, a plastic container with lid or clean gallon glass jar, etc., may suffice. For longer preservation, try a 4–5 gallon (18~22.5 *l*) plastic tub with cover, such as sold at bakeries.
* A plastic table-top pickle-maker has a screw spring core and simplifies pickle making, especially the process for making instant-type pickles.

DROP LIDS
* The drop lid should fit flat on top of pickles. Wooden drop lids are commercially available, but one can be easily made with clean smooth sturdy wood or with a solid ½ inch (1 cm) thick piece of polyethylene.

WEIGHTS
Improvise weights or buy. Cover crock with layers of plastic wrap then place weight on top.
* Fill a teapot full of water.
* Use a clean, washed rock or stone pebbles placed in a plastic bag. Some families even go "rock" hunting.
* Plastic-covered concrete weights are sold for pickling use.
* A large, clean brick encased in a heavy plastic bag can be used.
* For light weight, use several plates piled up.
* Use your imagination!

WEIGHT SPECIFICATIONS
* Weight needed on *tsukemono* varies depending upon the vegetable. For example, leafy greens need weight about ¾ of the weight of vegetable. Later change to about ⅓-½ weight of vegetable. For the more watery vegetable you need a heavier stone.
* For pickling eggplant, use a weight equal to at least weight of vegetable. After water has extruded, change to about ½ weight of vegetable.
* Dense vegetables such as *daikon* and carrot need a weight at least 1⅓ to 1½ weight of vegetable. Later switch to a weight about ⅔-¾ weight of vegetable.
* If there is reduced salt in your recipe use a heavier weight. Place weight so it will evenly compress vegetable.

STERILIZING JARS
Wash jars in hot suds and rinse in scalding water. Put jars in a large pot and cover with hot water. Bring water to a boil, covered, and boil jars for 15 minutes from the time that steam emerges from cooking pot. Turn off heat and let jars stand in hot water. Just before they are to be filled, invert jars on a clean kitchen towel to dry. Jars should be filled while still hot. Sterilize jar lids for 5 minutes.

USEFUL MEASUREMENTS

1 teaspoon = 5 cc
1 tablespoon = 15 cc
1 cup = 240 cc

Weight converted from volume

	Level measurements		
	1	1	1
	teaspoon	tablespoon	cup
water, vinegar, *sake*	5 g	15 g	240 g
shoyu, mirin	6 g	18 g	288 g
salt (pickling)	5 g	15 g	240 g
sugar (granulated)	5 g	9 g	144 g
miso, kneaded *kasu*			
(*sake* lees)	6 g	18 g	288 g

Sometimes it is simpler to estimate quantities by eye/hand measurements. Here are some practical gauges for such approximate measurements.

Hand measurements of salt

1 handful = 3 tablespoons
1 fistful = 2 tablespoons
1 pinch (with 3 fingers) = ½ teaspoon
1 pinch (with 2 fingers) = ¼ teaspoon

Eye and hand measurements of vegetables

1 medium carrot, 4 inches (10 cm) long = 7 oz. (200 g)
1 head Chinese cabbage (*hakusai*) = 4.4 lbs. (2.2 kg)
2⅜ inch (3.5 cm) diameter × 12½ inch (32 cm) long *daikon* radish = 4.4 lbs. (2.2 kg)
1 Japanese cucumber = 3½ oz. (105 g)
1 Japanese eggplant = 3½ oz. (105 g)
1 medium-size turnip = 9 oz. (270 g)
1 large cabbage leaf = 3 oz. (90 g)
2 inch (5 cm) diameter × 1½ inch (4 cm) long *daikon* radish = 2½ oz. (75 g)
heaping handful minced vegetables = 3½ oz. = 100 g
thumb-size ginger root = ⅓ oz. = 10 g

Note: To make pickling brine, add 2 teaspoons salt to 1 cup water.

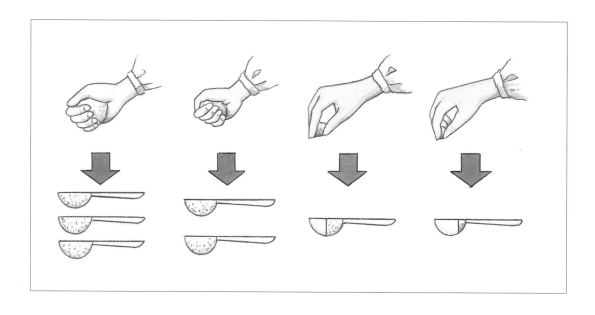

POINTERS FOR BETTER PICKLES

* 1 cup of well fermented old *nuka-doko* blended with new assists fermentation of a freshly prepared *nuka-doko*. Mix well.

* The addition of flavors to *nuka-doko* will improve taste. Use *konbu* from stock preparation. Dry *konbu* gives flavor as well as absorbs excessive liquid in *nuka-doko*. Red chili pepper or *sansho* seeds improve flavor. If *nuka-doko* gets stiff and hard add some beer, but not too often, about every 4 or 5 days.

* *Nuka-doko* will get moldy due to insufficient stirring, extensive temperature rise, insufficient salt, excessive hardness or softness. Scrape away the moldy surface ½-¾ inch (1~1.8 cm) thick on top. Transfer the healthy portion below to a clean container. Clean the moldy pickling container with detergent and dry in the sun. Give the lid the same cleaning treatment.

Be sure to remove all vegetable pieces in the old *nuka-doko* and place back in the clean container. Do not pickle immediately but wait 3–4 days, stirring *nuka-doko* in the morning and in the evening. Then it will be ready for pickling again.

* To prevent mold on *nuka-doko*, place a sterilized dishcloth, squeezed well, on top of *toko*. Cover surface with clear plastic wrap and put a lid on. Keep in refrigerator in summer and at room temperature in other seasons.

* When *miso-doko* is watery, place in a pyrex pot. Knead it. Cook with low heat until liquid has evaporated. Spread out on a platter to cool. Return to pickling container. If flavor is lost, add more fresh *miso*.

* If *nuka-zuke tsukemono* tastes sour and the color is not clear, this is due to insufficient salt or excessive fermentation.

Add 1 cup fresh *nuka* and 1–3 teaspoons salt to harden *nuka-doko*. Let stand 3 days, stirring

up and down twice a day to expose *nuka-doko* to the air. Do not pickle vegetables in the meantime. The sour pickles can still be utilized. Put in a container with a tight lid and keep in refrigerator. Serve as *kakuya* (minced pickles), adding flakes of dried bonito, crumbled *nori* (laver), thin strips of green *shiso* leaves and grated fresh ginger.

* Place a double thick plastic wrap layer between the jar lid (if not vacuum seal type) and jar rim. This prevents salt corrosion of the metal lid. It will be easier to twist open, too.

* DO NOT USE ALUMINUM FOIL in preparation of *tsukemono*. The acidity and saltiness of the pickles react chemically with foil. Poisonous to your health.

* To insure good safe eating, store *tsukemono* in the refrigerator if no other directions are given. Consume within several days to 1 week except for highly salted types.

* Sugar for pickling should be granulated sugar, unless other sugar is specified.

* Salt for pickling should be coarse pickling salt, unless other salt is specified.

* Use Japanese soy sauce (*shoyu*) rather than Chinese in these presentations to achieve best results.

The aroma and flavor of natural *shoyu* contributes to making food delicious. A few drops on *tsukemono* will make the sharpness more mild and appetizing. This is the result of *shoyu's* lactic acid content.

* Substitute for plum vinegar:
Umeshibori (plum juice) available at health food stores.. Or use pickling liquid from *umeboshi*-ginger pickle.

* If less than 3% salt in ratio with vegetables is used, it will take longer for liquid to ooze out. If weather is warm, *kira* (whitish scum) grows easily in liquid and pickles will most likely turn sour.

As a general rule, the weight placed on top should equal the weight of the vegetables being pickled. This will help liquid to be drawn out. If less salt is used, try a weight heavier than the vegetables.

* Experiment with vegetables not suggested in the recipes. Try lotus root, button mushrooms, red radishes, cherry tomatoes, various Asian greens, etc. Each one will have a different density, so adjust your marinating period to suit each vegetable.

* To help *takana* or similar ingredients release more liquid, place them in a large plastic bag after washing and drying. Trample with clean soxs on. This breaks down the cells and water will be released faster.

* If *rakkyo* is too sour, transfer pickling liquid to a pyrex pot. Add appropriate amount of water, salt and sugar to suit your taste. Boil and cool. Pour over *rakkyo*. Place a weight on for 2–3 days.

An alternative way to treat sour *rakkyo*: drain pickle and place in a solution of *shoyu*. *Shoyu* should be diluted with 20–30% of *konbu* stock. The pungency of the sourness will be softened. Do a small batch at one time.

Usually *rakkyo* is pickled in salt first, then in sweet vinegar. If pickled directly in sweet vinegar with no presalting, the *rakkyo* will remain crisp longer. However, this is not advisable for long storage. Use soft *rakkyo* minced in tartar sauce or as a relish. Reserve pickling juices from *rakkyo* and use in salads or reuse for brief marinating of onions, cucumbers, etc.

* Use whole *daikon* for pickling, rather than sliced, minced, etc., although a whole one may have to be cut into sections to fit into pickling container. This results in more evenly flavored *daikon*.

* To prevent *takuan* from looking anemic, add dried persimmon or orange peels for savory color and natural sweetness. Before *daikon* season arrives, dry and save fruit peels when fruits are consumed.

* If a vivid yellow color to *takuan* is desired, gardenia seeds can be used. Soak seeds in water to soften and crush to pieces with hands. Add while combining *nuka* and salt.

What can you do with salty *takuan* or other *tsukemono*? Here are some ideas for delicious dishes.

* Cut *takuan* into thin strips. Combine with cucumbers and carrots cut into julienne strips. Rub all together so salt from *takuan* will penetrate the other vegetables.

* Slice *takuan* thin. Rub slices in water to remove salt, and squeeze well. Fry with 3 tablespoons oil per 2–3 cups *takuan*. Season with red chili pepper, 2 tablespoons *shoyu*, 2 tablespoons *sake* and 1 teaspoon *mirin*. Boil down. Stir all the time until liquid is absorbed. Add a little sesame oil as you remove from stove. Keeps at least a week.

* Mince the salty *tsukemono*. Soak in water to remove salt before serving. Serve with some shaved dried bonito sprinkled as a garnish, or season with *shoyu* or mayonnaise.

* Use *tsukemono* as an ingredient in cooking. The salty, fermented *tsukemono's* distinctive flavor soaks in with other vegetables to make for a sophisticated taste. Pickles with advanced lactic fermentation are especially good used as ingredients for cooking.

Part I
Traditional
Tsukemono

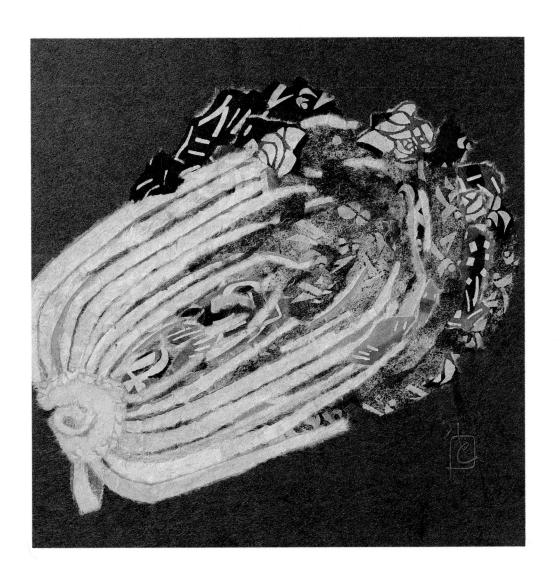

PICKLED CHINESE CABBAGE
(*Hakusai-zuke*)

Hakusai is the Japanese name for Chinese cabbage. This version uses a reduced amount of salt.

2 heads *hakusai*, approximately 11 lbs. (5 kg)
3/4 cup salt
10 cups water
2/3 cup rice vinegar
2–3 red chili peppers, seeded

Dry whole heads of *hakusai* outside in the shade unwashed, with bottom side up, for 2 days so leaves become pliant and limp. Wash. Remove outer leaves that appear bad (2–3 leaves). Save these leaves for end of recipe.

Split head into 4 parts by cutting head lengthwise from base to half the length of head with a knife. Split remaining upper portion by hand.

Cutting all the way through with a knife tears the leaves. Repeat to make quarters.

Sprinkle a handful of salt into base of your container. Place quartered *hakusai* sections evenly with cut surface upwards. Place base and leaf ends alternately in layers. Sprinkle salt on base section. Repeat as you do each layer. Place red chili peppers as you desire between layers.

Sprinkle more salt on upper portions, since salt gradually sinks to the bottom.

When all *hakusai* has been lined up, sprinkle balance of salt on top layer. Place removed outer leaves (saved from start of this recipe) on top as a sort of lid.

Place a drop lid and weight on leaves. Weight should be at least equal to weight of original *hakusai*.

Combine vinegar and water and pour between drop lid and wall of container. Never pour directly over *hakusai* since salt will wash away to the bottom. This vinegared water draws juices from *hakusai*. If started in the morning, by lunch juices will be drawn out. Reduce weight so juices will just cover drop lid. Ready to eat in about

1 week. This is a mild pickle and not for long preservation. It should be eaten early. Store in refrigerator, covered, for no more than 1 month.

Note: For a small family: Cut ¼ head of *hakusai* into 6–8 parts and wash. Place in a zip lock heavy plastic bag. Sprinkle salt evenly. Press bag to remove air. Tie with rubber band if not a zip lock bag. Place bag into a container. Cover with a drop lid and weight. Put in refrigerator overnight and it should be ready to eat in a day or so.

USES FOR *HAKUSAI TSUKEMONO*:

1. Rinse *hakusai tsukemono* and chop up. Add to stir-fry dishes, soups, spaghetti, etc.
2. Prepare your favorite meat loaf recipe reducing the salt. Make into loaf. Rinse *hakusai* leaves. Wrap around meat and braise with a sauce prepared from *shoyu*, sugar and *mirin* as seasonings. Slice and serve.
3. Use *hakusai tsukemono* as a wrapper for a rice ball. Rice ball can have salted *shiso* buds or toasted sesame seeds mixed together.

SMALL EGGPLANT IN BRINE
(*Nasu no Shio-zuke*)

Tiny Japanese eggplants have a beautiful appearance, with their vivid bluish purple color. If color is faded, the vegetable is old and past its prime. Rusty nails were traditionally used to retain color, however, in this modern age every nail is galvanized or plastic coated. Healthwise, this is for the better. Soaking in brine removes bitterness often found in eggplant.

15–20 small Japanese eggplants (see note below)
4 tablespoons salt
5–6 nails (optional)
Extra salt for rubbing eggplants
Fresh green *shiso* leaves (optional)

Boil 5 cups water and the 4 tablespoons salt. Transfer to a pickling container. Add nails, if used. Cool down. Wet your palms and sprinkle additional salt on hands. Rub each eggplant, leaving stem calyx as is. Soak eggplant in brine. Put on a drop lid and a weight. The eggplant should be all immersed in brine, as color will fade if exposed to air.

Ready to eat in 24 hours. To serve, float whole eggplant in water with crushed ice chunks for an artistic presentation. Add fresh green *shiso* leaves cut in strips floating on top.

Note: Western eggplant (medium size) can be substituted. Cut into sixths lengthwise, unpeeled. Use less salt in this instance since there will be more cut surfaces for salt to penetrate.

This pickling brine can be used for pickling 3–4 times more.

FRIED EGGPLANT

(Nasu no Kimpira)

This demonstrates how salted eggplant can be used in cooking.

Best to use the less salty-type of eggplant *tsukemono*. Goes well with *sake*.

Cut salted eggplant into bite-size pieces. Soak in a very weak brine of 4 cups water with 1 tablespoon salt for about 10 minutes. Squeeze dry. This removes some saltiness from the vegetable.

Sauté eggplant with a little salad oil. When oil has been absorbed, add equal parts of *sake*, sugar and *shoyu*. Boil down, stirring constantly, until liquid has all evaporated. Do not scorch. At the very end, a drop of sesame oil will enhance the flavor. If desired, one or two chili peppers will add zip.

PICKLED PLUMS
(*Umeboshi*)

This is a less salty method for making an old favorite. *Umeboshi* can be utilized in various dishes. Byproducts are white plum vinegar and leaves of red *shiso* in the *umeboshi*. They have a wide range of uses.

Umeboshi is nature's Alka Seltzer. It has been classed as a tonic aiding digestion; the acidic salty *umeboshi*, once eaten, alkalizes in your digestive system. A fabulous cleansing effect. When I travel I always carry a small jar of *umeboshi*. It has saved many a day! I mash a pickled plum and mix with hot water or green tea. It helps an upset stomach rapidly. And, *umeboshi* does not spoil. Keeps for a long period stored in the refrigerator.

Pickling in salt:
2½ lbs. (1 kg) green-yellowish plums, or sub-stitute green-yellowish firm apricots
Salt—use 10–15% of weight of *ume*

The salt in *umeboshi* is usually 20% of the weight of the plums, but in this adaptation the salt is reduced to 10–15%. Less salt does not necessarily mean a shorter preservation period. With the salt absorbed uniformly, *umeboshi* can keep 1 year. For more certain preservation increase the leaves of red *shiso*, which prevent mold with their natural preservative perilla aldehyde. Cover plums with sufficient leaves.

Select quality, faintly yellow *ume*—not green, hard plums nor ripe, sweet ones. Plums gathered on the West Coast in late June may be too late, although it depends on your location. They are available from very late May into mid-June in Japanese food stores. Despite the fact that these are called *ume* (plum), they are really a species of apricot (*Prunus mume*).

There are many kinds of *umeboshi*, but two types predominate. The popular red style contains red *shiso* leaves; the Kanto style is amber colored and contains no *shiso* leaves. There is a flavor difference.

Basic method for both styles:
Spread plums on a bamboo tray and keep in a well-ventilated place for 2–3 days. They will turn more yellow and are ready to be pickled. To remove the harshness, soak in water to cover for 10 hours. They will become somewhat soft. Spread out on a bamboo tray and drain lightly. Transfer into a pickling container while still wet. Sprinkle with salt. Let stand 2 days. Turn upside down once a day until some liquid is extruded. Place a drop lid or saucer over plums to prevent plums from swelling up. Place a heavy weight over the top. Wait 4–5 days so the salt will penetrate better. If making Kanto-style pickled plums, just cover the container and store it in

a cool place until the end of July.

To make red-style *umeboshi*, the next step is to add salted red *shiso* leaves to the plums. See next page.

WHITE PLUM VINEGAR

This very concentrated salty liquid which has oozed out of the salting plum procedure is called white plum vinegar. Keep it aside in a bottle. It can be used to prepare salted red *shiso* leaves. Diluted with water, it can be used for remedying physical fatigue.

RED PLUM VINEGAR

A month or so after adding salted red *shiso* leaves to *umeboshi*, a liquid results which is called red plum vinegar. It does not have the strong potency of white plum vinegar, but has sufficient sterilizing properties.

Make good use of the natural red color for pickling ginger, *daikon*, eggplant, cucumber, etc. This red plum vinegar can be added to rice for *sushi* and it improves the color and flavor as well as stimulates the appetite.

PREPARING SALTED RED *SHISO* LEAVES

Plums pickled with red *shiso* result in the *umeboshi* achieving a red savory color. *Shiso* also prevents spoilage. Furthermore, the flavor is enhanced with the red *shiso's* special aromatic flavor. Add a large amount of pickled *shiso* leaves to the pickled salted plums. If liquid is not sufficient add white liquor (*shochu*) to cover plums completely.

The red *shiso* harvesting season is June-July or later. Choose *shiso* leaves for *umeboshi* that are red on both sides. If green on the reverse side the *shiso* plant has cross pollinated with green *shiso* and the red color/flavor does not develop as well. If the red color has not soaked into the plums sufficiently within one year, the previous year's pickled *shiso* leaves can be added to enhance the color.

The following recipe can be used to prepare *shiso* leaves for *umeboshi* or for *yukari* (powdered *shiso*).

¾ lb. (330 g) fresh red *shiso* leaves
Handful salt

1. Use leaves of *chirimenjiso* (a red *shiso* variety—*Perilla frutescens*), red on both sides, with crinkled surfaces. The more vivid the color the better.
2. Rinse *shiso* in water well to wash away sand and dust. Pick leaves off stems and drain well. Put in a large bowl or *suribachi* (earthenware mortar). Sprinkle a handful of salt over *shiso* leaves.
3. Squeeze leaves with great pressure and a black liquid will ooze out. Squeeze well and discard juices. With insufficient strength in squeezing the black liquid will not come out and harshness will be left in *shiso*.
4. Return leaves to bowl. Pour white plum vinegar over them.
5. Press down on leaves until red liquid comes out. To get a true vivid red color do a good job as per direction #3.
6. Spread and separate the leaves over salted plums (page 23). The leaves will turn the plums red naturally.
7. Pour red liquid which comes out of step #5 over leaves.
8. Place a drop lid and a weight on leaves to soak plums completely in liquid. Cover container and let stand in a cool place until the end of July.

HOW TO DRY PICKLED PLUMS (*Doyoboshi*)

After plums have been pickled, they will keep longer if they are allowed to dry. Plums that are exposed to the air for 3 days and 3 nights will not become moldy.

Open-air method:
At the end of July, remove plums from pickling liquid and spread them out on a bamboo tray to expose to the sun. Turn plums over peri-

odically with clean hands. Let stand all night to expose to the night dew. If it rains, bring inside and repeat process another time. Continue this process for 3 sunny days and nights, turning plums over periodically. The skin of the plums will become smooth. Plunge plums into pickling liquid and immediately take out and store them in a covered container in the refrigerator.

If you are fearful of too much salt, plunge plums into white liquor or boiled and cooled *sake* instead of pickling liquid. In either case, the point is to keep the plums in a wet, soft condition.

Both amber Kanto-style and red *shiso*-style pickled plums can be dried in this manner. When drying red-style plums, remove leaves and plums from the pickling liquid. Squeeze the leaves well, and spread both leaves and plums flat on a bamboo tray. After drying, put plums back into pickling liquid and spread leaves on top of them. Replace lid on jar.

Kanto-style *umeboshi* should never be returned to the pickling liquid, as this may cause

plums to mold or blacken. Place Kanto-style pickled plums in a container without crushing them, and cover it. Store in refrigerator or in a cool, dark place.

Bottle method:

This time-saving method can be used only with red *shiso*-style plums that have been pickled in a glass jar. Loosen lid of pickling bottle enough to allow air inside. Expose bottle to sunlight for 3 days and 3 nights. Then tighten lid and store jar in a cool, dark place. This method leaves plums more plump than the open-air method.

CRUNCHY PLUMS
(*Kari-kari Ume*)

This recipe is a Western adaptation. The *ume* has an interesting crunchy texture and is sweet as opposed to the sour common *umeboshi*. Measurements are purposely vague since this recipe is almost fail proof. One can substitute unripe green apricots picked about mid-June while faintly yellow but still very hard. If you can get the Japanese type *ume* they are ready about the end of May depending upon the weather and locale.

Pick over *ume* and remove with a toothpick any piece of stem still left on the fruit. Soak in water overnight. This will remove dirt and sediment from *ume*.

Wash *ume* thoroughly. Drain well. Place in a bowl. Cover moderately with pickling salt and place a heavy weight on top of *ume*. Leave until water rises and covers *ume*. Let stand 24–30 hours. Remove weight and discard liquid, which is white plum vinegar, or save for other uses.

Make a small slit in *ume* and remove seed (optional) or leave whole. In a clean sterilized jar, layer *ume* and prepared *shiso* leaves (see method at end of this recipe). Cover with white granulated sugar. Repeat ending with sugar. After 7–10 days water will come out. Taste. Add more sugar if necessary. Repack in clean sterilized canning jars. Seal and refrigerate. Some more liquid will ooze out but not that much.

Preparation of *shiso* leaves: Wrap a teaspoon of sugar in each red *shiso* leaf and rub between your palms until juices start to flow. As soon as the juices become reddish, place with *ume*. If *ume* are large, they can be individually wrapped in *shiso* leaves, layered and covered with sugar.

Note: *Kari-kari ume* has a tendency to ferment easily even if kept refrigerated. You can drain the liquid and boil briefly, cool and replace in the refrigerated jar. This helps to prevent fermentation, mold or softening. Since *shiso* acts as a natural preservative, use plenty. And, besides, it is very tasty to munch on.

DARK RED COLORED *SHISO* (*Yukari*)

mixed with other ingredients to make a fine condiment. Can also be mixed with other *tsukemono* for flavor. Try sprinkling on top of soup.

Use salted red *shiso* leaves (recipe #1 page 24). Squeeze leaves firmly and spread them loosely on a flat bamboo basket to expose to sun until completely dried. A nylon netting or cheesecloth can be placed on top to prevent insect/dust from contaminating *shiso*. If you have a home dehydrator it is the simplest and cleanest method for drying *shiso* quickly. Crush dried leaves with a knife or a mortar/pestle.

Powdered, salted red *shiso* leaves can be used in many ways. Especially tasty over hot rice or

Store in an airtight can or bottle to prevent moisture absorption by the dehydrated *shiso*.

SWEET PLUMS
(Honey *Umeboshi*)

Another variation for *umeboshi*. This is sweet/salty and not sour like the traditional *umeboshi*.

3 gallons green *ume* or apricots
1¼ cups rock salt
Red *shiso* leaves
Pickling salt
2 lbs. (500 g) honey

Select green-yellowish *ume* which are firm and hard. Clean *ume* of all stems and soak overnight to remove dirt. Drain.

Mix rock salt and *ume*. Mix well each day.

Allow to soak for one month. Drain and save this white plum vinegar for other uses. Put salted plums in the shade for 3–4 days to shrivel and dry out.

Wash fresh red *shiso* leaves and rub with pickling salt. Squeeze firmly until black juices flow. Discard. As soon as juices turn reddish, leaves are ready to use. Alternate layers of *shiso* and plums. Top with salted red *shiso* leaves. Leave in a cool dark place for 2 months. Drain again, save liquid for future use. Add honey. Keep stored for one month without disturbing jar.

A MONK'S FAVORITE PICKLE
(*Takuan-zuke*, Reduced Salt and Sugar)

This *tsukemono* using *daikon* radish is a favorite of Japanese. Commercially sold *takuan* are often too sweet or too salty and some are not pickled with *nuka*. This low salt and sugar version has good flavor.

13 lbs. (6 kg) dried *daikon*—about 12–13 large *daikon*

¾ lb. (360 g) salt—6% of the weight of the dried *daikon*

⅔ cup brown sugar

1¾ lbs. (800 g) fresh *nuka*

5 or 6 dried red chili peppers

Dried persimmon, orange or apple peels, if desired

1 piece dried *konbu*

Dry and save peels from fruit to add special flavor. Hang whole *daikon*, including leafy top, to dry under the eaves or other shaded area out-side. Dry until *daikon* can be bent into a U-shape. Cut off tops together with a little portion of *daikon* so the tops will stay together. Tear dried peels of fruit. Slice *konbu* thinly. Mix salt, brown sugar, chili peppers, *nuka*, fruit peels and *konbu*.

Sprinkle two handfuls of this mixture about ¾ inch (1.8 cm) thick on bottom of a crock. Place *daikon* along side wall of crock. Then add more toward center. When one layer of *daikon* is packed, sprinkle *nuka* mixture to cover. Repeat layering. When all *daikon* has been packed, put tops of dried *daikon* in every opening. Make sur-face flat. Cover entire surface with tops of *dai-kon*, sprinkling remaining *nuka* mixture over top. Sufficient amount of *nuka* should be left over from layering process.

If *daikon* or tops are protruding from crock press them down with all your might. Put on a drop lid, a little smaller than crock. Then place a

28

weight 2 or 3 times heavier than dried *daikon* on the lid.

As salt penetrates *daikon*, the surface will lower. Remove weight and cover with a plastic sheet for dust protection. Return weight immediately and keep crock in a cool, dark place.

About 14–20 days after pickling, liquid will increase. Once liquid comes up to the drop lid

reduce weight equal to weight of dried *daikon*. Let stand a month to mature.

In removing *takuan* to serve, remove tops of *daikon* around edges. Put aside. Remove *daikon* from outer edge. Refill gaps with tops again to prevent deterioration of flavor. Cover surface with tops and *nuka* again. Press hard and put drop lid back on.

RICE BRAN PICKLES (*Nukamiso-zuke*)

With tender loving care, *nukamiso* improves with age and rarely deteriorates. Families have been known to maintain their *nuka-doko* for generations. Rice bran mash pickling base is used in this type of *tsukemono*. Every family has a favorite recipe and flavor. The fermentation stage is very overpowering; however, as the bed is used over and over a certain aroma pleasant or otherwise will evolve. The rice bran bed must be stirred daily. To protect hands from odor, cover them with disposable plastic gloves or use a wooden spoon to stir. The best flavors derived from a rice bran pickling base are achieved when it is made in a large quantity and used over and over. Affectionate and persistent care of the *nuka* bed is vital.

Nukamiso-zuke is a nutritious and healthy pickle. Vitamins of the vegetable are fairly well

retained and, by using rice bran mash, the vitamin B_1 and calcium content increases in proportion to pickling time. Not as salty as you might think.

Preparation of the *nuka-doko* (also called *toko*), a rice bran pickling base:

2½ lbs. (1 kg) fresh rice bran (*nuka*)—choose the fresh raw rice bran; it will ferment better

1 cup salt

1 thick slice white bread

2 cloves garlic, peeled and sliced thinly

6 cups water

Fragments of vegetables to fit a cotton bag 6 × 8 inches (15 × 20 cm) and top tied with a rubber band

Dried chili peppers (optional)

Konbu (kelp), cut into 1 inch (3 cm) strips (optional)

The pickling container can be enamel, plastic or a pyrex glass pot. The main point is that it must be salt and acid resistant.

Photo descriptions:

1. Put fresh *nuka* and salt in a large bowl. Add bread torn into small pieces, and garlic

2. Make a hollow in center of *nuka*. Pour in ⅔ of the measured water. Mix all ingredients uniformly with your hands plunged deep into the bowl.

3. Mix thoroughly. Pour in remaining water a little at a time. Do not make mixture too soft.

4. When consistency is somewhat softer than bread dough the *nuka-doko* is finished. The condition of the *nuka* allows for different absorption of moisture.

5. Transfer this *nuka-doko* to a pickling pot.

6. To make *nuka-doko* mature and result in delicious pickles it is important to do some preliminary pickling. Use peels and tops of *daikon*, peels of carrots, outer leaves of regular head cabbage or Chinese cabbage, tops of turnips, etc. Cut into pieces. Place in a cotton bag and tie top with a rubber band.

Place bag at bottom of pickling pot. After about 12 hours when vegetables are pickled take out and replace with more peels, tops, etc. Repeat this process with more peels about 3 times. These pickled peels do not have to be discarded. Slice thinly and add to meat/fish stir fry dishes. Now your *nuka-doko* is ready for whatever vegetables you choose. After vegetables have been immersed be sure to cover top with a clean cloth to prevent contamination with dust, but still allow for air flow.

PICKLING TIMES AND VEGETABLES SUITED FOR *NUKA-DOKO* PICKLING METHOD

The pickling times suggested here are for spring weather; in winter it will take 20–30% more time, and in summer only half the time.

EGGPLANT

1. Rub salt over surface of tiny Asian-type eggplants. Leave calyx on top. This prevents deterioration of color.
2. Slit a cross mark in base of eggplant. Do not cut too deeply.
3. Place some *nuka-doko* into slash for absorption of flavor.
4. Place eggplant lengthwise into bottom of *nuka-doko* with slashed end up. Ready to serve in about 8 hours.

KOHLRABI or CHAYOTE SQUASH

1. Select 2–3 inch (5~8 cm) diameter kohlrabi, since larger ones may be porous. Cut off tops. In the case of chayote cut right through the large soft seed, since it is edible.
2. Trim tops, removing part of hard surface of kohlrabi top. Often fibrous.
3. Peel kohlrabi thickly to remove net-like tissues near surface.

4. Place kohlrabi cut into quarters into *nuka-doko*. Best to eat in about 10 hours. Can be lightly or heavily pickled. A different taste to vary your vegetable selection for *nukamiso-zuke*.

CARROTS

Peel carrots for good appearance. Cut a slash at the top. Put *nuka-doko* in slash. Put carrot lengthwise into pickling bed. Vegetable is dense so it will take longer to ripen . . . about 12 hours.

DAIKON

Do not cut *daikon* in half lengthwise since flavor penetration will be uneven. Cut crosswise in 3 inch (7.5 cm) sections. Peel may be left on if it is not stained.

CELERY

Cut off thin stalks at top and leaves. Remove strings and cut into 4 inch (10 cm) lengths. Place lengthwise in *nuka-doko*. Do not pickle more than one day since it will get stringy and tough. Thin stalks and leaves can be pickled briefly (less than 24 hours) by placing them in a cotton bag.

TURNIP

1. Cut off roots.
2. Peel surface near tops if stained with mud and has poor appearance. Otherwise leave unpeeled.
3. Turnip should be pickled whole. Takes about 20–30 hours. If you want to speed pickling process, make a half-inch deep slash at the bottom before placing in *nuka-doko*. Tops can also be pickled and will be ready in about 8 hours.

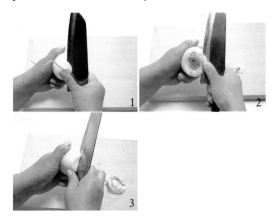

SHIRO-URI

1. *Shiro-uri* has a tendency to get sour, so do not pickle too long. When cut in half, it will take about 3–4 hours to mature. For evening use, place *shiro-uri* in *nuka-doko* in mid-morning.
2. Cut *shiro-uri* in half. Scrape seeds and pulp with a spoon. Rub salt lightly throughout surface. Place *shiro-uri* with cut surface up in *nuka-doko*. Make only as much as needed at one meal.

HEAD OF CABBAGE

1. Separate leaves one by one. Cut off hard ribs.
2. Spread a little amount of *nuka-doko* between 2 leaves. Press together.
3. Roll up paired leaves from one side to the other. Try not to break leaves. If rolling is difficult leave unrolled.
4. Place 3 deep into *nuka-doko* crosswise. Ready to serve in 10–15 hours. Leaves placed in morning can be served at dinner.

SQUASH (*KABOCHA*, ACORN, BUTTERNUT, ETC.)

1. Small fresh *kabocha* grown near top part of vine is excellent for *nukamiso-zuke*. Peel skin.
2. Place squash in *nuka-doko*. Best to eat within 15 hours. Strongly pickled squash is also tasty. To speed pickling, slice thinly and put in *nuka-doko*.

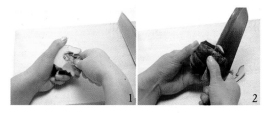

TINY JAPANESE CUCUMBER

Size should be about ¾ inch (1.8 cm) diameter × 5–6 inches (12~15 cm) long. To serve for breakfast or lunch the next day there is no need for special preparation of cucumber. Keep buried in *nuka-doko* overnight. To speed pickling rub outside peel with salt and place in *nuka-doko*. Ready to eat in 2 hours.

SUGGESTIONS FOR OTHER VEGETABLES TO USE IN *NUKA-DOKO*

Okra, green pepper, zucchini and other summer squashes, asparagus. Trim hard ends and blanch in hot water several minutes. Cool with cold water. Drain and wipe off moisture). Add to *nuka-doko*. Also try broccoli, lettuce, small green tomatoes (these pickle in about 36 hours), ruta-bagas, parsnips, hard green papaya, etc. Experiment! Dried chili peppers and *konbu* (kelp) cut into 1 inch (2.5 cm) strips can be added to *nuka-doko* for additional flavor.

IMPORTANT TIPS TO ACHIEVE BEST FLAVOR AND EXCELLENT RESULTS

To keep *nuka-doko* active: Stir up every day, putting hands deep toward the bottom, at least once a day or once after every meal in summer. By stirring up *toko* well it exposes it to the air. This helps the fermenting action of lactic bacteria which forms the characteristic flavor of *nukamiso-zuke*.

Nukamiso will result in smelly hands, but well-kept *nuka-doko* will never have an unpleasant odor or become bad. Use plastic bags over hands to protect from odor. Always keep the *toko* top flat and keep inside of container clean. A dirty container attracts mold. Prepare a towel to be used exclusively for wiping as necessary. Keep towel on a plate placed on the container top.

When removing pickled vegetables from *toko*, shake off *nuka*. Never squeeze, especially in the case of greens, for it will make *toko* watery. Stir *toko* from bottom to top. Add new vegetables to be pickled and flatten surface of *toko*. Clean inside of container with a towel.

When *nuka-doko* becomes watery, wash *toko* towel, squeeze firmly and spread open over *toko* (see photo above). Place cloth cover over container to protect *nuka-doko* from contamination and dust. Plastic wrap is not good. Air is vital for *nuka-doko*.

Absorb most of excess liquid with towel and

remove it. Do not try to extract liquids completely since flavor will also be removed.

In winter keep *toko* somewhat watery and soft or vegetables will take a long time to be pickled.

When *nuka-doko* is running low and watery do not absorb the liquid with a cloth but add more *nuka* to *toko*. Together with *nuka*, mix a little bread, torn in pieces, into *toko*. After a trial pickling and tasting, add more salt. Everyday use will make *toko* run low and short of salt. Add *nuka* to *toko* in same way as above once or twice a month according to frequency of use or amount of pickles made.

When *nuka-doko* tastes sour, remove all vegetables and add ½ to 1 cup dry mustard and some salt. During hot days sprinkle a small amount of mustard over *toko* and mix. However, mustard stops fermentation so never use it when you add *nuka* or bread.

REVIVING SOUR *NUKA-DOKO*

Sometimes after a long suspension of use, especially in summer, *nuka-doko* gets puffy and light when you feel it. *Toko* is contaminated at this point. It still can be saved even if it is moldy except in extreme cases. Remove all vegetables. Add 1 cup salt, 10 cups *nuka* and at least ½ lb. (220 g) to ¾ lb. (330 g) dry mustard to the "sick" *toko*. Mix well and expose to the air thoroughly. Stir up *toko* at least 3 times a day. In 3–4 days it will be ready to use again.

REFRIGERATOR METHOD

Use this simplified *nuka-doko* method when you do not have time to care for the *toko*, or when you need only a small quantity of pickles. There is no contamination in summer if kept in refrigerator.

1 lb. (500 g) raw rice bran (*nuka*)
7 tablespoons salt
2 half-inch (1.2 cm) slices of white bread
1 clove garlic, peeled and sliced thinly
3 cups water
1 tablespoon plain yogurt
Fragments of vegetables in a cotton bag 4 × 6 inches (10 × 15 cm)
3–4 tablespoons dry mustard

Prepare this *nuka-doko* in the same way as standard recipe except for addition of plain yogurt and mustard. Do not forget to stir *toko* daily.

Mix fresh *nuka* and salt in a large bowl with your hands deep in bowl bottom. Add bread torn into fine pieces. Add garlic slices. Pour ⅔ of measured water and combine all ingredients well. Pour remaining water little by little, watching stiffness of mixture. It should be somewhat harder than the earlobe.

Mix plain yogurt to facilitate fermentation. Transfer mixture to a container with a matching lid appropriate for refrigerator storage. Soak minced vegetable fragments in a cloth bag in *nukamiso-doko* (pickling bed) for two days. Repeat this twice. Keep at room temperature for a week. Then transfer to refrigerator in lidded container. Let stand 2 weeks. Mix in mustard. Now it is ready to use as a pickling base.

When you do not pickle daily and cannot care for *nuka-doko* for several days, remove all fragments of vegetables completely. Add a little salt and 3–4 tablespoons mustard to *nuka-doko*. Transfer to a heavy polyethylene bag or container to keep in refrigerator. You can place *daikon* or carrots in the bag during storage since they can be over seasoned and still be tasty.

Another method for long time preservation of your *nuka-doko*: Remove all fragments of vegetables. Transfer to thick polyethelene plastic bags, exclude air and tie ends firmly. Place bags in freezer. This will deactivate *toko* for several months.

In both methods, with *toko* returned to pickling container you can resume your *nuka-zuke* process at any time.

BASIC *MISO-ZUKE*

Low-salt types of *miso* are gaining favor for health reasons. *Miso* (fermented soy bean paste) adds a rich flavor and is becoming popular in America. If kept airtight, *miso* will keep a long period in the refrigerator.

½ cup medium-salty *miso*
2 tablespoons *sake*
1 tablespoon *mirin*

The traditional method places salted vegetables into the *miso* bed. This recipe seasons vegetables well without extra salting. The saltiness varies according to *miso* type. Use a medium-salty *miso* for best results.

This pickling bed is suitable for vegetables of varying densities. Celery will be ready to eat in 5–6 hours; kohlrabi, turnip, or *daikon* will take about 10 hours. Vegetables placed in the *miso* bed in the evening will be ready for lunch the next day.

Add *sake* to *miso* to soften it. Mix well. Add *mirin*. If this pickle will be eaten to accompany *sake*, do not make it too sweet. Transfer ⅓ of the prepared *miso* into a flat container. Spread 2 layers of cheesecloth over *miso-doko* pickling base. This will make removal of pickled vegetables easier. Place celery and kohlrabi (cut in small pieces) in a layer. Spread cheesecloth over vegetables. Spread balance of *miso* mixture all around. Flatten surface with a spatula. Cover with cheesecloth and put a cover over container. Keep in refrigerator in summer and at room temperature in winter.

This *miso-doko* pickling base can be used repeatedly. If mixture becomes too watery due to juices from vegetables, add 2 teaspoons sugar and ¼ teaspoon powdered red chili pepper to substitute for *mirin* and *miso*.

The overused *miso-doko* can be used as flavoring for *miso* soup in combination with lots of other ingredients.

If you desire to preserve this *miso-doko*, place in a flat container with a lid. Keep in refrigerator in summer and at room temperature in winter.

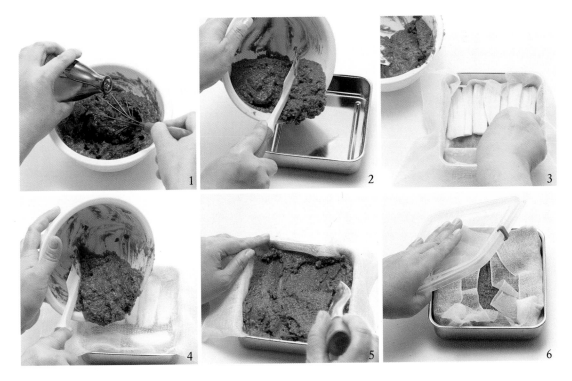

1   2   3

4   5   6

Variations for preparing *miso-doko* are as follows:
1. Add *shoyu* to *miso-doko*.
2. Sweeten *miso-doko* by adding *mirin* and sugar.

3. Use *Saikyo* (Kyoto-style sweet, white) *miso* as a *miso-doko* base for fish or meat.

SPICY PICKLED CELERY
(Celery *Miso-garame*)

This is a refreshing *tsukemono*—
not so salty.

3 ribs celery with strings removed,
   cut into 3 inch (7.5 cm) lengths
3 tablespoons red *miso*
1 tablespoon *mirin*
1 tablespoon *sake*

Place celery in clean jar. Cover with mixture of *miso, mirin* and *sake*. Let stand about 15 minutes. Cut marinated celery into bite-size pieces. Serve with some fresh shredded celery leaves sprinkled on top.

   Leave some of the *miso* paste on celery for more flavor. When celery is well-seasoned remove *miso* paste completely.

Variation: Stir-fry the fresh celery for an instant and cover with *miso, mirin* and *sake* paste. Serve immediately.

MELON PICKLED IN *SAKE* LEES (*Shiro-Uri Kasu-zuke*)

Shiro-uri is a melon of the gourd family and looks like a very fat, long, white cucumber. It grows easily in the home garden.

Many pickling recipes used by the Issei pioneers in America were approximate measurements. This recipe is an exception and has been used by a friend for many years with great results. It has accurate measurements!

20 lbs. (9 kg) *shiro-uri* (net weight after seeds have been removed)

2 lbs. (900 g) rock salt
1 lb. (450 g) pickling salt } mix together

Cut *uri* in half lengthwise. Remove seeds. In a large crock or plastic container layer *uri*, sprinkle salt. Repeat until all used.

Cover with a drop lid. Place a heavy weight on top, such as a clean rock. Leave for 3 days and 3 nights. A lot of water will come out.

Drain. Wipe each *uri* well with a clean cloth. Dry in shade for 24 hours. Keep covered with a cheesecloth, or a paper can be substituted.

7 lbs. (3 kg) *sake* lees (*kasu*)
9 lbs. (4 kg) sugar

Mix *kasu* and sugar well. Layer *uri* with *kasu* mixture, ending with *kasu*. Cover with a lid.

In about 10 days it will be a little watery, so mix from top to bottom and all the *uri* will result in the same color and taste. Repeat in about a month. These steps will result in crunchy *uri kasu-zuke*. Should be ready in about 6 months. Be patient. Store in a cool, dry place undisturbed.

To keep it a lighter color, place in refrigerator before a year has passed, or earlier. Some people like to keep *uri* for several years and it darkens. A very large plastic pail with a lid, sold by bakeries, makes an ideal container for this amount of pickling.

SAKE LEES PICKLING BASE (Kasu-zuke-doko)

This pickling base is stored over the hot months to age. It gets sweeter and the paste will slowly turn brownish.

4½ lbs. (2 kg) *sake kasu* sheets (*sake* lees)
½ cup *shochu* (white liquor)
½ cup water
Bamboo leaves or heavy plastic wrap
Sugar (optional) for added flavor

Sake lees sheets are available fresh from the end of the year through February. Otherwise use frozen ones. Prepare *kasu* pickle base during this season and you can use it when vegetables are available later in the year. *Sake* lees keep well in the freezer in a plastic bag.

Place *sake* lees sheets, crushed into pieces, in a pyrex or plastic container. Press and flatten with hands. (See photos on page 38.)

Blend white liquor and water. Pour some over *sake* lees. Press. Repeat until all water/liquor mixture is used. Cover with plastic wrap to exclude air. Place a weight on top of wrap. Cover all with a thin plastic wrap and put in a cool, dark place until autumn. About September, it will be tasty and flavorful due to fermentation.

Take out whatever amount is needed. If desired, add sugar or *mirin* to *toko* for extra flavor. If large clean bamboo leaves are available, they can be used to cover *kasu-doko* during the fermentation period. They act as a sterilizer and an air insulator, preventing mold bacterial development. (See photos on page 38.)

Suggested vegetables for *kasu-zuke*: daikon, cucumber, eggplant, celery, chayote, jicama. The vegetables should be heavily salted and allowed to stand prior to immersing in *kasu-zuke-doko*.

KOJI/MISO/KASU TSUKEMONO BASE

A way to use left-over rice. This results in very tasty pickles.

1½ cups *koji*
3 cups left-over rice
1 cup *miso*
1 cup *sake* lees (*kasu*)

4 tablespoons salt
1 tablespoon sugar
½ cup water

Mix all ingredients to form a thick paste.

To pickle: Cucumbers can be cut in half and dunked into this paste and be ready to serve in 1 day. Try eggplant, *daikon*, etc. After using 4–5 times, replenish pickling base ingredients a little at a time. This *toko* will last at least 3 months with care. Keep in a cool place.

3-5-8 PICKLES (*Sagohachi-zuke*)

These pickles are named after the ratio of 3–5–8 (pronounced *sa, go, hachi*) preserving mixture of salt, *koji* and uncooked rice. The following recipe is an adaptation with less salt. This base can be used over many months as long as it is refrigerated.

BASIC *SAGOHACHI* MIXTURE

8 cups raw short-grain rice
5 cups rice *koji*
2 cups salt

Wash raw rice and place in a heavy pot with about 20 cups hot water. Cook covered until very soft, about 50 minutes, to make a soft rice porridge. Stir well. Allow to cool down to 140°F (60°C).

Add rice *koji* to the cooked warm rice. Mix with a rice paddle or spatula constantly until mixture is well blended. The *koji* yeast must incubate for 24 hours, so wrap container with towels and place over a heating pad set on low.

After this fermentation has been completed it will result in a soupy mixture called *ama-zake* (sweet *sake*). (See note below.)

To continue with the *sagohachi* base, mix in salt. Allow to stand about a week. Mixture will have a bland taste since salt will be absorbed into the mass. Prepare a clean pickling container and keep covered in a cool dark place, or better, keep refrigerated.

To use base, take out appropriate amount needed for each pickling use. Suggested vegetables: cucumbers, small eggplant, *daikon*, zucchini, squash, turnips, rutabaga, cabbage, chayote, etc. Experiment.

Cut vegetables into chunks or slices, i.e., cucumber 2 inch (5 cm) slice, and coat well with the *sagohachi* base. Do not overcrowd. The pickled vegetables will be ready in less than 1 day, if thinly sliced first. Otherwise it will take longer. Stir the pickles once a day and add more vegetables. Add more base if necessary. Serve crisp vegetables without washing off pickling base.

Sweet *Sake* (*Ama-zake*)
This basic rice/*koji* concoction can be served as a non-alcoholic drink: Put 1 part base with 1½ to 1¾ parts water in a saucepan and bring just to a boil. Season with a dash of salt, pour into warm tea cups and dab a bit of grated fresh ginger on top.

DAIKON RADISH PICKLED IN *KOJI* (*Bettara-zuke*)

A classic Japanese *tsukemono* famous in the Tokyo area. Also called *Asa-zuke*. The name is derived from the viscosity of the *daikon* surface when pickled by the authentic method. This recipe is a simplified version.

1 large *daikon*, peeled thicker than usual for
    good flavor penetration
Salt (about 4% weight of *daikon*)
1 cup *ama-zake* base, see page 40

Cut *daikon* into lengths to fit pickling container. Peel and cut in half lengthwise. Place *daikon* pieces in container and sprinkle with salt. Weight lightly and let stand 1–2 days.

    Discard liquid. Drain *daikon* in a strainer. Spread a small amount of *ama-zake* base in clean container. Put in *daikon* pieces in a layer. Spread more *ama-zake* base on them. Repeat, ending with *ama-zake* on top. Cover with plastic wrap and weight lightly. Ready in 2–3 days. When serving do not wash off clinging rice kernels. Serve in thick slices to enjoy the unique sweet juicy taste.

Note: The resulting *daikon* peelings can be julliened and cooked in *shoyu* and sesame oil or dehydrated for later use (*kiriboshi-daikon*).

    Additional sugar can be added to the *ama-zake* base if one prefers a more sweetened taste. A dried red chil pepper, seeded, will give this zip. Best to consume within a week. Keep refrigerated.

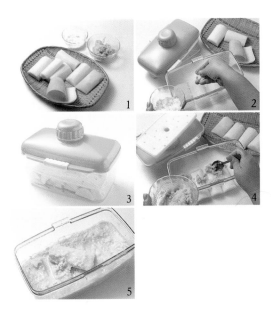

41

BASIC SALTED SCALLIONS (*Rakkyo-zuke*)

Rakkyo is a kind of Japanese shallot or scallion, usually available in May and June. A good substitute is the tiny whole pearl boiling onion. *Rakkyo* served in the salted manner described below is delicious, and this is also the basic recipe for Sweet *Rakkyo*, *Rakkyo* in Honey and *Rakkyo* in *Shoyu*.

2⅓ lbs. (1.2 kg) raw *rakkyo* with roots and stalks
4 cups rice vinegar
4 cups water
4 tablespoons salt or 6% of weight of *rakkyo*

Clean *rakkyo* well but retain roots and stalks. Put *rakkyo* in a clean pickling container. Do not cut both ends of *rakkyo* to prevent heart from slipping out, and so there will be less salt absorption. Add water and vinegar to cover *rakkyo*. Add salt.

Shake container to mix salt with liquid. Put an interior lid or saucer on top. Weight down with pebbles or small stones placed in a bag, as shown in photos 4 and 5 on page 42.

In about 10 days *rakkyo* will be ready to eat. If mold occurs, wait until it cakes and throw out.

Sufficient pickling solution prevents *rakkyo* from touching any mold.

Before serving, cut off both ends of *rakkyo*. If too salty, soak in a weak brine (4 cups water and 1 tablespoon salt) for 5–6 hours to remove excess saltiness.

SWEET SCALLIONS (*Rakkyo Amazu-zuke*)

This is a sweetened version of *rakkyo* using the basic *Rakkyo-zuke* recipe.

2.2 lbs. (1 kg) salt-vinegared *rakkyo*—see page 42
Pickling solution:
    2 cups sugar
    1 cup *mirin*
    1½ cups rice vinegar
    1 or 2 red chili peppers (optional)

Scrub prepared *rakkyo* in water to peel off outer skin roots and stalks. Change water several times. Taste and if too salty soak in a weak brine (4 cups water and 1 tablespoon salt) to remove saltiness.

Boil sugar, *mirin* and rice vinegar. Cool. Place prepared *rakkyo* in sterilized jar and pour in pickling solution. Let stand 10 days. If desired, add 1 or 2 red chili peppers with seeds removed.

SCALLIONS IN *SHOYU* (*Rakkyo Shoyu-zuke*)

Another use for basic *Rakkyo-zuke* recipe.

2.2 lbs. (1 kg) salt-vinegared *rakkyo*—see page 42
Pickling solution:
    1½ cups *shoyu*
    1½ cups rice vinegar
    ½ cup *sake*
    ½ cup *mirin*

4-inch piece *dried konbu* for flavor
2 red chili peppers (remove seeds)

Scrub prepared *rakkyo* in water to peel off outer skin, roots and stalks. Place *rakkyo* in a sterilized jar. Put pickling solution into jar and shake jar up and down. Ready to eat when *rakkyo* develops a good brownish tinge.

SCALLIONS IN HONEY (*Rakkyo Hachimitsu-zuke*)

Another variation of basic *Rakkyo-zuke* recipe.

2.2 lbs. (1 kg) salt-vinegared *rakkyo*—
    see page 42
Pickling solution:
    2 cups rice vinegar
    1 cup sugar
    1½ cups honey
    red chili peppers (seeds removed)
    lemon slices (optional)

Scrub prepared *rakkyo* in water to peel off outer skin roots and stalks. Change water several times.

Taste and if too salty soak in a weak brine (4 cups water and 1 tablespoon salt) to remove saltiness.

Mix together pickling solution and *rakkyo*. Transfer to sterilized jar. Cover and shake up and down every few days. Ready to eat in 15 days.

SPECIAL SCALLIONS (*Rakkyo Shio-zuke*)

This is a Westernized simplified version of sweet *rakkyo* for easy preparation. Some directions are contrary to the conventional pickling method, but the results are delicious!

Enough *rakkyo* (Japanese scallions) or small white pearl onions to fill a gallon jar
1½ cups pickling salt

Trim top and root section of *rakkyo* close to bulb. Remove thin outer skin. Wash carefully and drain. Salt and let stand a week stirring twice a day. Do not place any weight on top. Remove *rakkyo* and rinse quickly in cold water. Drain. Place drained *rakkyo* in a clean jar or crock.

Pickling solution:
    3 parts rice vinegar
    3 parts sugar
    3 parts water

Boil above ingredients together and cool. Pour over packed *rakkyo*. Cover with a lid. Store in a dark, cool place. A gallon jar with a good seal is excellent. Shake it a few times every day to pickle all the *rakkyo* thoroughly. After a month, drain *rakkyo* and remove to a clean jar or crock. Add a fresh new batch of pickling solution. After another month or so the *rakkyo* should be ready to eat. Refrigerate.

GREEN PEPPER PICKLES

A very simple recipe to follow. It calls for green peppers, but red and golden types may be added for variation. Such an array of pepper colors is now available—even orange, purple, white and lilac ones.

Enough fresh green peppers to fill 4 quarts (4.5 l)
Pickling solution:
    4 cups cider vinegar
    2 cups water
    1 box (1 lb., 450 g) brown sugar
    ½ cup salt

Slice cleaned green peppers in thick pieces. Discard all seeds. Pack into sterilized jars. Bring vinegar, water and brown sugar to a boil. After dissolved, add salt slowly. Bring back to boiling point and pour over peppers packed in jars. Seal. This brine is enough for 4 quarts of pickles. The addition of a clove of garlic and one red chili pepper in each jar will make for a tasty flavor.

Since Japanese *shoyu* (soy sauce) is produced by a slow fermentation of soybeans, wheat, salt and lactic bacteria, it is an excellent base for *tsuke-mono*. Use the light all-purpose style *shoyu* in these recipes. Do not substitute Chinese or other types of soy sauce—the flavor is different.

ASSORTED PICKLED VEGETABLES (*Fukujin-zuke*)

Fukujin-zuke is customarily served with Japanese curry rice along with *rakkyo* and red pickled ginger, as chutney is used in other mid-Eastern style curries. This is also good with plain rice, served steaming hot.

1 lb. (500 g) assorted vegetables such as *daikon*, carrot, lotus root, well-salted cucumber, eggplant, beans, celery, etc.
Salt as needed
3 tablespoons salted *shiso* seeds
Preliminary pickling solution:
  ½ cup *shoyu*
  ⅓ cup *mirin*
  a little *sake*, if desired
Regular pickling solution:
  1 tablespoon sugar
  ½ cup *shoyu*
  ½ cup *mirin*

Peel *daikon* and carrot, cut in quarters lengthwise and slice thinly across. Sprinkle lightly with salt. Put 2–3 plates on top and let stand 2–3 hours.

Peel lotus root. Slice the same size as *daikon*. Pour slightly vinegared hot water on slices.

Cut in half lengthwise Japanese cucumbers which have been heavily salted and slice thin. Slice several kinds of salted vegetables, such as eggplant, etc., in the same manner as *daikon*. Drain all vegetables well. Put into a wide mouth jar. Pour preliminary pickling liquid on vegetables. Add salted *shiso* seeds. Mix vegetables up and down with chopsticks so they absorb liquid evenly.

Let stand 3 days until the liquid is absorbed by vegetables and its amount decreases. Prepare regular pickling liquid in the following manner: Put measured sugar in a small saucepan and cook over low heat. Add a little water to caramelize sugar. Pour measured *shoyu* and *mirin* in pan. Cook and melt the caramel. Cool down. Squeeze and discard liquid from soaking vegetables in the preliminary stage. Pour cooled caramelized pickling solution over vegetables. It should just cover the vegetables when you press down on them. Ready to eat in 2–3 days.

Toasted sesame seeds and chili pepper pods can be added, if desired, when caramelized pickling solution is added.

SHIBA-ZUKE

Shiba-zuke is purplish-red color and the *tsuke-mono* is more on the sour side. True Japanese style uses *kamonasu* (eggplant grown in the Kyoto area), *uri* (a melon of the gourd family) and red *shiso* leaves.

INSTANT RED PICKLES (Instant *Shiba-zuke*)

½ large *daikon*
2 Japanese cucumbers
2 Japanese eggplants
} cut into thin julienne strips

Rub with 1 tablespoon salt and let stand overnight. Wash vegetables quickly and drain.

Soak in a mixture of the following:
⅓ cup red plum vinegar from *umeboshi*
1 teaspoon sugar
MSG (optional)
10 red *shiso* leaves, cut in strips
5 knobs *myoga*, thinly sliced

In one day, vegetables will be soaked to a purplish red color and ready to serve.

NATURAL RED PICKLES (*Shiba-zuke*)

7 small Japanese eggplants
7 small Japanese cucumbers, salted
5 buds pickled *myoga*
2 tablespoons white plum vinegar
2 tablespoons red plum vinegar (or substitute rice vinegar flavored with 2 minced *umeboshi* plums)
1½ tablespoons rice vinegar
1 tablespoon minced leaves of red *shiso* from a jar of *umeboshi* plums
1-1½ teaspoons sugar

Peel eggplant leaving strips of purplish colored peel. Cut in half and diagonally cut into ¼ inch (5 mm) thick slices. Place in a bowl with salt brine (2 cups water and 2 teaspoons salt) to remove bitterness.

Weight down with a saucer on top and a cup filled with water to prevent floating. Let stand 20 minutes.

Squeeze eggplant firmly. This process will prevent eggplant from floating in pickle mixture.

Prepare cucumbers with brine in a manner

similar to eggplants. Cut cucumbers in ¼ inch
(5 mm) thick slices. Wrap in a cheesecloth and
soak in water to remove excess salt. Squeeze
lightly.

Cut *myoga* pickled in salted vinegar into
halves. Then slice thinly lengthwise. Squeeze
lightly.

Mix eggplant, cucumbers, *shiso* and *myoga*.
Sprinkle with red plum vinegar, white plum vinegar and sugar.

Put this mixture in a pyrex bowl and place a
2 lb. (900 g) weight on top. Mix once or twice to
blend flavors. Ready to serve in 1 day.

FLOATING PICKLES (*Ukashi-zuke*)

A never-fail recipe because the vegetables are merely soaked.

2½ lbs. (1.1 kg) any combination of vegetables that you have on hand, i.e., turnips, cucumbers, carrots, *daikon*, cabbage, roughly cut cauliflower in florets, radish, broccoli, etc.
4 inch (10 cm) square piece dried *konbu*
2–3 red chili peppers

Pickling solution:
  6 cups water
  ½ tablespoon salt
  3½ tablespoons white plum vinegar or substitute lemon juice with extra salt added

In this recipe any vegetable can be pickled except greens, since they change color due to the acid in white plum vinegar. Combine several vegetables for an attractive combination of colors.

Peel turnips with tops cut off leaving about ¾ inch (1.8 cm) stalks. Cut cucumber into 1½-3 inch (4 cm—7.5 cm) long thick strips or slice crosswise.

Wipe *konbu* surface with a wet cloth squeezed tightly. Cut *konbu* into 1½ inch (4 cm) lengths and slice into thin strips.

Remove seeds of red chili peppers.

Prepare pickling solution. Put water and salt in a pan. Bring to boiling point then cool down. In hot weather, cool in refrigerator if necessary. Add white plum vinegar.

Mix cut vegetables, *konbu* and chili peppers together. Put in a wide mouth jar. Pour pickling liquid over vegetables. To prevent vegetables from floating, put a heavy-duty plastic sandwich bag filled with clean stones over surface. Solution should just cover bag.

In summer this will be ready to eat in 1 day, but it's tastier after 2 days since flavors will have matured. In autumn and winter it will take 3–4 days. White plum vinegar gives excellent flavor and body to this pickle, or use lemon juice with extra salt added.

This solution can be saved and used 2–3 times repeatedly, with the addition of more salt and vinegar. To use over again: Remove all pickled vegetables in jar. Add more salt to old liquid. Boil and cool down. Add more white plum vinegar. Do not mix old vegetables with new ones, or taste will be spoiled.

PICKLED GREENS (*Omi-zuke*)

Originally, discarded vegetables in the fields were used. This *tsukemono* is well known in the Yamagata area. Favored vegetables are *karashina* (mustard), *takana* (Chinese mustard) and other similar greens. Tops of *daikon*, carrots, stems of taro left in the fields after harvest were also utilized.

¾ lb. (330 g) salted greens such as mustard, *takana* or Italian rabe broccoli, *daikon* tops (salted, or pickled in *nuka-miso*)
1 6-inch (15 cm) length of salted *daikon* or *takuan*
½ carrot
Pickling solution:
    2 tablespoons *mirin*
    2 tablespoons *shoyu*
    1 tablespoon white plum vinegar

Tastiest if salted *daikon* leaves and stems are included, however, fresh *daikon* leaves can be substituted. Slice into 1½-inch (4 cm) lengths together with other pickled greens. Cut *takuan* (*daikon*) and carrot into quarters lengthwise and slice very thinly across.

Put above ingredients loosely into a cotton bag and tie ends. Place in a large pot of water to remove excess salt. Rub bag with hands and repeat 2–3 times. The fresh *daikon* greens will get good flavor transfer this way. Drain in a colander. Squeeze well and put vegetables in a bowl. Pour mixture of *mirin, shoyu* and white plum vinegar on top. If no white plum vinegar, soak one large *umeboshi* in a small bowl of water just covering the plum—use this water in place of the vinegar

Mix vegetables well to allow seasoning to penetrate. Place in a clean pickle-maker jar with liquid just covering vegetables. Screw lid on tightly. Ready in 1 day. You can keep 1 week in refrigerator.

Part II
Tsukemono
with
the
Seasons

RAPE BLOSSOMS

When rape blossoms (and other similar wild plants) of early spring with yellow flowers (*nanohana*) appear, we know "spring has sprung." Rape blossoms are not readily available in America to the general public, although commercially, rape seeds are used for the production of canola oil. A good substitute is wild mustard or Italian rabe broccoli.

RAPE BLOSSOM *TSUKEMONO*

1 lb. (450 g) rape blossoms and leaves
1 tablespoon salt

Prepare rape blossoms by removing any thick, hard stalks. Blanch in boiling water until just

wilted. Immediately take out and rinse in cold water. Squeeze water out gently.

Line neatly in a pickling container. Sprinkle salt and place a light weight on top. Ready to eat in 24 hours. Will keep 4–5 days with no additional care. This *tsukemono* can be preserved for a longer period by wrapping finished *tsukemono* in a zip lock bag and freezing. Will keep 2–3 months. Texture will be slightly changed.

How to serve:
1. Since this is very lightly salted, it can be eaten like boiled fresh greens, seasoned with a little *shoyu* and garnished with shredded dried *bonito* (*itogatsuo*).
2. Serve *natto* (fermented soybeans) seasoned with mustard and *shoyu* along with the greens.
3. Minced as a garnish for *oshiruko* (sweet *azuki* bean soup with *mochi*, rice dumplings).
4. Rinse *tsukemono* and add to soups.

51

PLUM AND CHERRY BLOSSOMS

This is an exotic way to preserve the exquisite beauty of spring—pickled blossoms served one or two at a time. Since the flowering season is so very brief what a wonderful idea to conserve the fragile beauty and to enjoy the delicate taste.

SALTED PLUM BLOSSOMS (*Baika-zuke*)

Salting plum blossoms is more difficult than salting cherry blossoms, but worth the try.

Remove seeds from *umeboshi* and pass flesh through a mesh strainer. Spread paste on bottom of a ceramic pot with a matching lid. Just before plum blossoms are in full bloom, pick and stick calyxes into the paste. Place lid on pot.

How to serve:
1. Drop a blossom into a cup of hot refined green tea and enjoy the aroma and flavor.
2. Put a blossom in a tea cup with *umeboshi* paste or a little salt. Fill with hot water and serve.

SALTED CHERRY BLOSSOMS (*Oka-zuke*)

Salt-preserved double cherry blossoms are most distinctive and add a touch of luxury in our "mad modern" world.

½ lb. (225 g) double cherry blossoms
2 tablespoons salt
Red plum vinegar (or substitute ¼ cup rice vinegar plus ¼ cup water)

Pluck double cherry blossoms half-opened and just before the full bloom stage. Those in full bloom are inferior in flavor. Use bunches of 3 or 4 clusters. Carefully remove stems.

Pickling process:
Put blossoms in a strainer and clean by shaking gently in water. Take out blossoms. Drain. Put in a pickling container. Cover them with salt. Weight down with a few plates or the like. Once liquid has come out, transfer blossoms to a strainer and drain. Put blossoms back into a clean jar. Pour red plum vinegar just to cover. Allow to stand a week. Drain them again in a strainer but save liquid.

Spread out on a flat basket and dry in the shade for 2–3 days covered with a cheesecloth. Put blossoms back into original liquid. Sprinkle a little salt and keep in a storage container in a dark, cool place. Blossoms will keep up to 3 months in this salt/liquid solution.

How to serve: As shown, use a blossom as a garnish for green tea or rice. Or put blossoms plain in a tea cup, then pour in hot water for a delicate tea.

SALTED CHERRY LEAVES

After blossoms fall from the cherry trees, pick young large leaves right away. The leaves harden and the color deteriorates as time passes. So hurry.

6–8 oz. (180~240 g) cherry leaves
4 tablespoons salt

Pickling process:
1. Wash leaves well. Drain gently in strainer. Place leaves evenly in a steamer and steam for 2–3 minutes.
2. Soak leaves in cold water for a moment and put in a strainer to drain. Put leaves in a container, sprinkling salt over them. Place a weight on top. The liquid comes up in a day. Transfer leaves to a storage container and keep. Leaves may be pickled without steaming. But to get better flavor and taste, steam them. Use for *sakura mochi*. (See next recipe)

RICE CAKE WITH *SHISO*
(*Sakura Mochi*)

A special rice crepe filled with sweetened *azuki* bean paste and wrapped with a cherry leaf. For centuries, this has been prepared especially for the Girls' Day Festival on March 3rd.

Soak 10 salted cherry leaves in water for half a day to remove excess salt.

½ cup all purpose or pastry flour
⅛ cup *shiratamako* (refined glutinous rice flour)
¾ cup water
1 tablespoon sugar
Red food coloring (a drop or two), if desired, added to batter
Oil for frying
An (sweetened *azuki* bean paste—see below)

Dissolve *shiratamako* in ¼ cup water. Add and mix flour, ½ cup water, and sugar to *shira-tamako*. Cover paste with a wet cloth. Allow to stand 30 minutes.

Use a lightly oiled heated skillet. Fry 10 oval-shaped pancakes (4 × 2⅓ inch; 10 cm × 6 cm size) over low heat. Do not brown. This will not take too long. Put *an* "log" on one edge of prepared oval pancake while in pan. Roll up carefully with help of a spatula. After 10 pancakes have been completely prepared, wrap a cherry leaf around each.

An (Sweetened Bean Paste)
Use a recipe for *an* from any general Japanese cookbook, or buy a can of *koshi-an* (sweetened bean paste). It is already sweetened and ready to use. You can store the balance in the refrigerator. Form into 10 tiny 2 inch (5 cm) long "log" shapes. Put aside until ready to use with pancakes.

GREENS

By using less salt, greens will remain a fresh bright color. However, this is not a suitable method for long preservation.

SALTED MUSTARD GREENS *(Takana Tsukemono)*

Use Chinese mustard greens with deep green leaves or use red leaf *takana*.

4½ lbs. (2 kg) *takana*
½ cup salt

Wash *takana*. Be sure to separate stalks at the base with hands. Drain. No need to dry.

Sprinkle a handful of salt in a pickling container. Pack some *takana* aligned in one direction and sprinkle more salt over them. Pack second layer of *takana* crisscross to first layer. Keep height of layers uniform. Sprinkle more salt on stems than on leaves. More salt should be on top layer than on the bottom.

When layering has been completed, sprinkle remaining salt over all. Place a drop lid and a 9 lb. (4 kg) weight on top of *takana*. Pour a little water around drop lid. Keep in a cool, dark place until liquid comes up. Reduce weight to 4½ lbs. (2 kg). If insufficient salt is used, *takana* will be bitter. Rinse before serving. This *tsukemono* should be

ready in 24–36 hours. Use within 10–14 days. Keep refrigerated.

Note: *Takana* mustard seeds are readily available on the seed stands. Very easily grown in the home garden. Besides preparing *tsukemono*, try the *takana* cooked with pork or chicken. Excellent flavor. A California idea: a few prunes or a fistful of raisins added to the salting process cuts the sharp salt taste. Discard before serving.

SALTED GREENS *(Mizuna Shio-zuke)*

This is a Japanese green seen more and more in American markets. It is also easily grown in the home garden. The tiny young tender slender leaves are excellent mixed in salads. Normally, when ready for market, it is sold as a large head similar to the way endive and chicory are marketed. Can be used for soups, stir-frys, etc.

Mizuna
Salt—use ratio of 3% weight of *mizuna*

Rub *mizuna* with about ⅓ of the salt to remove bitterness. Use balance of salt sprinkled on top of *mizuna*. Place a weight twice as heavy as *mizuna*. Once liquid has come up, reduce weight in half.

Place in a zip lock plastic bag and transfer to refrigerator. Best to eat in 4–5 days, since fermentation is rapid in hot weather.

GREENS AND CUCUMBER COMBINATION

Wash a salted *takana* leaf. Replace water 2–3 times to remove excess saltiness. Separate stalk from leaf portion. Slice both thinly.

Slice two small Japanese cucumbers thinly. Sprinkle a little salt over them and allow to stand 10 minutes until limp. Squeeze out juices. Combine cucumbers with *takana*. Sprinkle ½ teaspoon *shoyu* over combination, mixing until taste suits your palate. Serve.

If a lot of greens are already salted, you can enjoy a variety by making instant vegetable pickles mixed with salted greens. A dash of sesame oil gives good flavor and makes an excellent accompaniment to *sake*.

CURRY-FLAVORED *MIZUNA* AND CARROTS

Curry wakes up the flavors of these vegetables.

¼ lb. (120 g) *mizuna*
½ medium size carrot
2 teaspoons salt
1 teaspoon curry powder

1 tablespoon water
Toasted sesame seeds for garnish
Optional additional ingredients: bean sprouts, *konbu*, *wakame* or red *shiso* leaves

Wash *mizuna* well. Cut in 2 inch (5 cm) lengths with root base removed. Peel carrot and cut in 2 inch (5 cm) long fine strips. Put *mizuna* and carrot in a table top pickling jar. Sprinkle salt over all and rub gently. Screw down pressure on jar.

Let stand about 30 minutes. Drain liquid. Add curry powder dissolved in water and mix well. Wait 20–30 minutes until flavor has matured. Ready to serve.

To give added color, a small quantity of optional ingredients above can be added. Toasted white sesame seeds sprinkled on top will enhance this *tsukemono*.

CABBAGE

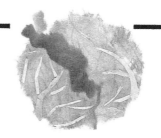

The versatile cabbage mixes well with a wide variety of vegetables and flavors, making it a useful ingredient for home pickling.

KNEADED CABBAGE
(*Momi-zuke*)

5 cabbage leaves, cut into ½-inch (1 cm) wide strips
2 inch (5 cm) carrot, cut into thin strips
1 fresh ginger, finely shredded
1½ teaspoons salt

Put cabbage leaves, carrots and ginger in a bowl. Sprinkle with salt and mix until wilted. Squeeze out moisture and serve in a small bowl.

CABBAGE, CUCUMBER AND GREEN *SHISO* *TSUKEMONO*

Green *shiso* tastes like mint, citrus and licorice, adding spiciness to the cabbage and cucumber.

3–4 large cabbage leaves, cut into ½-inch (1 cm) wide strips
2 Japanese cucumbers, thinly sliced
2 teaspoons salt
10 green *shiso* leaves
Red chili pepper, seeded and cut into rings

Put cabbage leaves and cucumbers in a bowl. Sprinkle with salt and mix. Wash and pile up *shiso* leaves one on top of another. Slice into thin strips. Mix with cabbage and cucumbers. Place a weight equal to 2–3 plates on top. Let stand 20–30 minutes. Squeeze out moisture and serve in a small mound. A few red chili pepper rings will enhance the flavor and make an attractive presentation.

AMERICAN CABBAGE *TSUKEMONO*

Japanese restaurants in America favor this method, since the pickle keeps well and it does not involve tedious work. This recipe is a favorite of a very creative American cook who shared it with me.

1 large head of cabbage
⅓ cup pickling salt
¾ cup sugar
3 cups water

Boil salt, sugar and water together and cool. Cut cabbage into quarters and remove core. Make vertical cuts ⅜–½ inches (9~12 mm) apart and rotate sliced cabbage ninety degrees to make similar cuts to produce bite-size pieces.

Place chopped cabbage in a clean gallon jar and pour cooled brine over all. Let stand at room temperature for 24 hours without any weight. This allows cabbage to ferment and achieve a slightly tart taste. Repack in clean canning jars and refrigerate.

Just before serving, rinse cabbage lightly to remove excess salt. Squeeze out water. This keeps 2 weeks or more refrigerated.

Note: To hasten pickling process: Put chopped cabbage in a large pan and sprinkle 1 teaspoon salt over. With both hands squeeze and push down gently just enough to "bruise" cabbage. Proceed according to above directions.

GINGER AND *MYOGA*

Both *myoga* and ginger are seasonal. They give variety to a diet and stimulate the appetite. Good as garnishes too. Outside of Japan, more and more ginger root is available in all grocery stores, and *myoga* can be found in Asian markets.

MYOGA IN SALTED VINEGAR

4½ lbs. (2 kg) small firm *myoga*
Salt (5% of the weight of *myoga*)
Pickling solution consisting of 1 part rice vinegar
   to 1 part water
Clean stones in a zip lock or cheesecloth bag
Bonito shavings for garnish

Wash *myoga* and drain. Snap off plant stem if too long. Pack *myoga* in a clean wide-mouth jar leaving a one-inch (2.5 cm) space at the top. Pour water half way up in jar. Pour vinegar just to cover *myoga*. One can increase the vinegar ratio if desired. Add salt on top of *myoga*. Tilt and rock jar gently to dissolve salt.

Wash small stones. Sterilize by boiling and let cool. Place in a cheesecloth, nylon net bag, or zip lock plastic bag. Tie ends if necessary. This will be used as a weight. Place bag evenly over *myoga* to prevent floating. Liquid should come just over the weight. Put on lid and keep in a cool dark place. Ready to eat in 3–4 days.

Garnish with a little dried bonito shavings.

GINGER IN SWEETENED VINEGAR (*Gari*)

This is most often served with *sushi*, in a mound on the side. It is nibbled between bites of *sushi*, to refresh the palate.

1 lb. (450 g) fresh ginger (select young ginger roots)
⅔ cup rice vinegar
¼ cup *mirin*
¼ cup *sake*
3 tablespoons sugar

Wash ginger roots well with a scrubber and place in boiling water for a minute. Boiling water removes offensive odors.

Combine vinegar, *mirin*, *sake* and sugar in a pan. Boil until sugar dissolves and allow to cool. Put ginger into a large clean jar. Pour pickling mixture over all. Sterilize small stones as in *myoga* recipe, page 58. This will prevent ginger from floating. Cover. Ready in 3–4 days. Keeps at least a month in refrigerator. A natural soft pinkish tint develops as it ages.

GINGER PICKLED IN PLUM VINEGAR

This recipe uses old sweet vinegared ginger which has passed its prime.

Slice ginger lengthwise and put into a pickling container. Put a weight over ginger and pour red plum vinegar just to cover. This pickle will keep a

long time.

Use as a garnish. The light red color adds brightness to dishes. Mixes well with seasonal *tsukemono* prepared from cucumbers, turnips, *daikon*, etc.

JAPANESE *SHISO* MINT

Shiso (*Perilla frutescens*) is available in both red magenta-purple leaf variety and a green leaf type. They are not interchangeable in recipes since the flavors are entirely different. *Shiso* is an annual herb and resembles an ornamental coleus plant. This plant with square stems is related to the mint family. Seed germination is about 3 weeks; it grows well in home gardens in California. Reseeds annually. But be sure not to plant red leaf *shiso* near green leaf *shiso* since there will be cross-pollination and flavors will not be true. Also root cuttings can be made easily in water. Seeds are available from Kitazawa Seed Co., 1111 Chapman St., San Jose, CA 95126.

The leaves, flowers and seeds are all usable in many ways. Leaves add spice to bean curd and are a garnish for *tempura*. The tiny seeds are also prepared as *tempura*, or pickled for a variety of *tsukemono*. Small green sprouting *shiso* is used for added zip to *sashimi* and *sushi*. The most well known use for the red magenta-purple variety, sometimes referred to as beefsteak plant, is in the making of *umeboshi* (pickled plum) and *tsuke-mono* such as *shiba-zuke*. The salted leaves are rubbed and rolled by hand to break open plant cell structure and a natural red dye explodes with the addition of plum vinegar.

Shiso contains a natural preservative called perilla aldehyde so it has a sterilizing property excellent for pickling.

Shiso is also very popular in Korea and is used in its cuisine for its medicinal qualities as well as for its taste.

SALTED GREEN *SHISO* SEEDS

Pickled green *shiso* seeds are tasty when mixed with rice or vegetables. Very good also mixed with different salted vegetables such as chopped cucumbers. Or remove salt by soaking in water and prepare as *tempura*. Photo shows fried seeds with stems intact, ready to be served as an accompaniment to *sake*. The seeds can be added to *natto* and cuttlefish.

½ lb. (225 g) fresh green *shiso* seeds (either with stems attached or seeds removed and stems discarded)
3½ tablespoons pickling salt

Soak green *shiso* seeds in lots of water overnight. This removes harshness and dirt around seeds.

Squeeze water out well from seeds. Sprinkle with salt (at least 20% ratio to the weight of seeds). Put in a wide-mouth jar with matching lid. Weight contents down with 4–5 small stones, sterilized and put into a cloth bag.

In the event you pickle seeds with stems, pour water just to cover when you place them in jar since this will fill up the opening around seeds and prevent color deterioration due to oxidation (contact with air).

SALTED GREEN *SHISO* LEAVES

Fresh green *shiso* leaves are familiar to many in America now, since Japanese foods have become popular. They garnish *sushi* and *sashimi* dishes and add a piquant touch. Green *shiso* is often grown commercially in hot houses, making it available year round.

1 lb. (450 g) fresh green *shiso* leaves
1 gallon (4 l) water
¾ cup salt

Wash green *shiso* leaves well. Pile up by tens one on top of another. Tie stems with cotton thread. Mix water with salt. Pour over *shiso* leaves. Place a wooden drop lid to prevent leaves from floating in the container. Let stand overnight. Drain leaves in a colander. Hold leaves between your hands and press firmly to squeeze out water well. Do not crumple leaves.

Sprinkle some salt on bottom of container. Put prepared leaves in layers and sprinkle more salt. Repeat until all leaves have been used. Press hard to exclude air. Weight down with a plate or

the like.

Keeps at least a year in refrigerator, with salting when necessary. To use leaves, wash quickly and wipe dry. Wrap around rice balls for a snack. Add minced leaves to other vegetables to make an instant pickle. Or add thinly sliced salted green *shiso* leaves to thinly sliced onions and ham, and season all with a salad dressing.

SALTED RED *SHISO* LEAVES

1 lb. (450 g) red *shiso* leaves with stalks
6¼ tablespoons salt

Pluck leaves from stalks and wash well. Pile leaves by tens with stem ends together and align neatly. Sprinkle salt over leaves and pour water to cover. Let stand 3–4 days. Discard black liquid which oozes out as you squeeze leaves together.

Place leaves in a clean jar. Pour white plum vinegar just to cover leaves. If no white plum vinegar is available, substitute same amount of vinegar with 5% salt dissolved in it. Place a weight on top. Leaves will become a red color. Use this pickled leaf as an ingredient for *shiba-zuke* or *yukari*. For other uses for red *shiso* leaves, refer to index.

VINEGARED RED *SHISO* LEAVES
(*Akajiso Senmai-zuke*)

250 fresh red *shiso* leaves
3⅔ oz. (110 g) salt
3¼ oz. (100 cc) white plum vinegar, see page 23

Wash *shiso* leaves. Bundle them by 20s, and bind lightly with thick thread.

Layer them in pickling container, and add 1 oz. (30 g) of salt, sprinkling some over each layer.

Place a drop lid and a 2½ lb. (1 kg) weight on them a night and day. Discard the black liquid that oozes out.

Place prepared leaves in a pickling container layer by layer. Add 2⅔ oz. (80 g) salt and the white plum vinegar, sprinkling evenly over each layer. Place a drop lid and a 5 lb. (2 kg) weight on them. Leave in a cool place for 1–2 months.

RICE CAKES WITH RED *SHISO* LEAVES
(*Shiso Mochi-Gashi*)

Salted red *shiso* leaves wrapped around a tiny ball-shaped *mochi-gashi* (glutinous sweet rice cake filled with *an*) is a delicious confection. This is a specialty of the Kyoto area. A very refined taste; goes especially well with green tea. Salty and sweet.

Sweetened red bean paste (*an*), see page 53
Salted red *shiso* leaves, see pages 24
½ lb. (250 g) *mochiko* (glutinous rice flour)
¼ teaspoon salt
¼ cup sugar
1 cup water
Rice flour or cornstarch

Form balls about ¾ inch (2 cm) diameter with sweetened red bean paste (*an*). Set aside. Drain salted red *shiso* leaves briefly. Lay out on a clean cloth to dry off while you prepare *mochi* balls.

Mix *mochiko*, salt and sugar together. Add water and stir to consistency of bread dough. Lay a wet cloth in steamer and place dough on top. Steam for 15–25 minutes. Poke dough with a toothpick and if it comes out clean it is ready.

Place dough in bowl. Pound and knead with a wet wooden spatula until sticky consistency. Remove from bowl and place on board sprinkled with rice flour or cornstarch. Pinch off dough about 1¼ inches (3 cm) in diameter. Flatten in palm of hand and place an *an* ball on top. Wrap dough completely around. Pinch ends together and shape into a small golf ball. Wrap a prepared salted red *shiso* leaf covering the entire ball with an overwrap of the leaf.

DRIED APRICOTS/RED *SHISO* CONFECTION

This is my analysis of a specialty of Northern Japan, where years ago I first experienced this marvelous combination and fell "in love" with the tantalizing flavors. Sweet, tart and salty. This, again, is a way to use salted red *shiso* leaves (page 24).

Dunk dried (in leathery pliable stage) apricot halves in some of the plum vinegar that pickled salted red *shiso* leaves are soaking in. Or, if you happen to have a jar of *umeboshi* with lots of

shiso leaves you can remove some of that liquid and use. Sprinkle sugar on apricots. Spread out a moist salted *shiso* leaf and wrap a sugared apricot in it. Repeat until all apricots are used. Set aside in a single layer for ½ day, covered, in refrigerator. Flavors will co-mingle. Apricots should not get mushy with too much moisture from the *shiso* leaves. Try to keep dried apricots still chewy. This goes well with green tea as a confec- .tion. This is not for long preservation—only a few days in refrigerator.

CABBAGE/*UMEBOSHI* ROLLS

A very unique way of using *umeboshi*. The combination is most appetizing and attractive.

4 large cabbage leaves
Salt
8 green *shiso* leaves
4 *umeboshi*, seeds removed, mashed
Several pinches dried bonito flakes
1 tablespoon *shoyu*
1 tablespoon *mirin*
4 slices lemon, for garnish

Parboil cabbage briefly to soften. Drain. Sprinkle with salt while still hot. Cut away hard ribs of cabbage. Blanch green *shiso* in boiling water briefly. Mix *umeboshi*, bonito flakes, *shoyu* and *mirin*. Set aside. Put *shiso* leaves on top of cabbage leaves. Spread *umeboshi* mixture on top of *shiso* leaves. Roll up. Cut cabbage rolls into slices. Place slices attractively on a plate, cut side up, with a garnish of lemon slices.

PICKLED SALMON ROLLED WITH *SHISO* LEAVES (*Sake Shisomaki-zuke*)

3 slices of medium-salted salmon
3 tablespoons vinegar
15 fresh green *shiso* leaves, salt lightly or moderately
1 knob of fresh ginger root
1 onion
½ of a lemon

Cut salmon into bite-sized pieces. Pour vinegar on them and let stand 30 minutes; salmon will

keep longer.
Slice onion and ginger into thin strips. Soak *shiso* leaves in water to remove salt.
Spread *shiso* leaves open, and place salmon, onion and ginger on them in even amounts. Fold into square shapes.
Lay salmon rolls in a container. Put lemon slices on them. Weight down lightly and let stand in refrigerator. Ready to eat in 2 hours.

GARLIC

Garlic has been used by Asian peoples for centuries for medicinal purposes. Garlic cloves pickled add flavor and are not strong smelling. You will be surprised to find pickled garlic served with meals, with tea as a snack, as appetizers, etc. Try it on the side with your meat dishes.

GARLIC WITH SOY SAUCE

Garlic cloves
Shoyu

Remove thin skin from garlic cloves. Put into a clean jar and pour *shoyu* just to cover. Ready in 2–3 weeks. You can replenish with more garlic as it is used up. This pickling liquid can be further utilized for preparing *chaofan* (fried rice), pilaf and spaghetti or other dishes using *shoyu*.

GARLIC WITH BEAN PASTE

Garlic cloves
Red *miso*

Remove thin skin from garlic cloves. Soak in red *miso*. To speed process cut garlic cloves in half. In this case *miso* will have a strong garlic flavor. (This flavored miso can be used for preparing certain fried dishes as your secret seasoning). When serving, pickled garlic cloves should have some of the *miso* adhering to them. Different.

GARLIC WITH HONEY

Garlic cloves
Honey

Remove thin skin from garlic cloves. Put into a
clean jar. Pour honey just to cover. If fresh garlic
clove skins are hard to peel, remove only outer
skin and leave root portion intact to be removed
later. This pickle will ferment easily so keep in
refrigerator, especially during summer.

FLAVORFUL GARLIC *TSUKEMONO*

1 garlic bulb, separated into cloves, peeled and
    thinly sliced
¼ lemon, thinly sliced
Green *shiso* leaves, cut crosswise (*mitsuba* leaves
    can be substituted)
Pickling solution:
    ¼ cup white wine
    ⅔ cup rice vinegar
    1 teaspoon curry powder
    1 teaspoon salt

Soak all together for 2–3 days. Consume as soon
as ready since flavor is at its prime.

CUCUMBER

Cucumbers should either be lightly pickled as sort of a salad or heavily salted for long preservation. Cucumbers pickled halfway are not very tasty.

PICKLED CUCUMBERS CHINESE STYLE

The pleasant taste of this instant pickle stimulates the appetite lost by the heat of summer, and sesame oil helps you to recover strength. A good accompaniment to *sake*.

6 Japanese cucumbers or 2 Western cucumbers
1 tablespoon salt
1 stalk green onion, cut 1 inch (2.5 cm) segments
1 knob fresh ginger, sliced into thin strips
2 red chili peppers, sliced into thin strips
1 tablespoon shaved dried bonito, toasted and crumbled (optional)

Pickling solution:
   3 tablespoons vinegar
   5 tablespoons *shoyu*
   1 tablespoon sesame oil

Sprinkle salt over cucumbers which have both ends cut off. Let stand 30 minutes. The cucumbers will become pliant. Line them on a cutting board and beat with the flat blade of a knife to make cracks on skin. Cut into 1 inch (2.5 cm) lengths. Put cucumbers, onions, ginger, chili pepper and dried bonito together. Pour pickling solution over all. Allow to stand 2–3 hours at room temperature and serve. This recipe can also be refrigerated for 1 day.

QUICK CUCUMBER AND EGGPLANT

2 Japanese cucumbers
2 Japanese eggplants, cut in half lengthwise
2 inch (5 cm) square dried *konbu*
Shoyu
1 tablespoon *sake*

Make diagonal slashes on eggplant peel. Soak in water to remove bitterness. Make deep, thin slashes on cucumbers and then cut into bite-size pieces. Drain eggplant and cut into bite-size pieces.

Combine eggplant, cucumber and *konbu* in a clean jar. Pour *shoyu* up to half the height of vegetables. Add *sake* and mix all ingredients by shaking jar up and down a few times with the lid on. This will be ready to eat in 2 hours.

CUCUMBER COMBINATION (*Matsumae-zuke*)

6 Japanese cucumbers
salt
2-inch (5 cm) piece *dashi-konbu*, cut into thin strips with a scissors
Red chili peppers with seeds removed, cut into thin rings
Shoyu
MSG (optional)

thick piece of quality *dashi-konbu*. Cut as thin as possible. You may wish to add a small amount of carrot, cut into thin strips, making this pickle most colorful.

Rub cucumbers with salt. Cut off ends and slice into bite-size pieces. Mix cucumbers with *dashi-konbu* and chili peppers in a bowl. Pour *shoyu* to a level just a little short of the height of mixture. Add MSG if desired. Let stand half a day at least. Mix occasionally.

The pickling *shoyu* retains the delicate flavor of *konbu* and the solution can be used again for 2–3 more times if kept refrigerated. Choose a

EGGPLANT

To retain the vivid purple color of eggplant, rub well with salt or alum. Except for the long preservation type *tsukemono*, pickle only what you can consume within a reasonable time.

INSTANT EGGPLANT *TSUKEMONO*

5–6 Japanese eggplants, cut crosswise into
  ¼ inch (5 mm) thick slices
1½ tablespoons salt
1–2 *myoga*, minced, or substitute fresh ginger

Put eggplant in a large bowl and sprinkle salt on. Put a plate on top to weight down. Allow to stand for 20–30 minutes. Once brown liquid has oozed out rinse eggplant, changing the water 3–4 times. This removes harshness. Drain well.

Mix *myoga* with eggplant which has been squeezed well to remove water. Serve in a small bowl. If desired sprinkle a little *shoyu* to improve flavor.

EGGPLANT 3-5-8
(*Nasu Sagohachi-zuke*)

This method can preserve eggplant for a long time. The name comes from the ratio of the ingredients for the pickling paste. See page 41 for further information on 3–5–8. This recipe employs a shortcut by using a commercially prepared 3–5–8 packaged mix.

15 Japanese eggplants with calyxes attached
3 cups water
½ cup salt
½ cup commercially prepared 3–5–8 pickling
  base mix, or see page 40 for homemade *sago-hachi* mixture.

Put water, salt and calyxes cut off from half the eggplants in a pan. Boil them and cool.
  Put all the eggplants in this cool solution.

Place a drop lid on them. Let stand 2–3 days, and salted eggplant will be ready for the next step. Prepare ½ cup commercial 3–5–8 pickling mix to 15 Japanese eggplants. Sprinkle mix on the bottom of a pickling container. Place salted eggplant in a layer. Sprinkle mix over them and repeat layers, ending up with mix. Weight down heavily.

It is better to eat this pickle early to enjoy the sweetness of the *koji* (in the 3–5–8 mix). If preserved longer, eggplant will become salty. If it is too salty, soak in water to remove salt prior to serving. Other vegetables such as cucumber, turnip, *daikon*, etc., are good substitutes.

MUSTARD EGGPLANT 3-5-8
(*Nasu Karashi Sagohachi-zuke*)

Usually the 3-5-8-*doko* is made from nonglutinous rice. But in Yamagata Prefecture it is made from glutinous sweet rice or unmilled brown rice (*genmai*).

8 cups glutinous sweet rice (*mochi-gome*)
5 cups malted rice (*koji*)
3 cups salt
2½ lbs. (1 kg) Miniature-size Japanese eggplants
½ cup mustard powder

In advance of pickling, prepare the 3-5-8-*doko*. Mix hot rice (cooked softer than usual) and loosened malted rice. Keep mixture warm for a night and it will become sweet due to fermentation. Add salt. Allow to stand 4–5 days, stirring mixture once a day. Allow it to stand another 10–14 days without stirring until it ripens.

Transfer this paste to a clean wide-mouth jar and keep at room temperature. Take out appropriate amount to pickle your eggplant.

Remove calyxes from Japanese eggplants.

Wash eggplants and drain. Place in a pickling container. Add mustard powder, mixed with water, to 2 cups 3-5-8-*doko*. Coat eggplant with the paste. Place a drop lid and a weight twice as heavy as eggplant (4.4 lb.; 2 kg). Cover container and wrap in plastic film to retain heat. Ready to eat in a day. For longer preservation after eggplant has soaked for 3 days, throw out liquid that has come out and soak eggplant again in new 3-5-8-*doko*.

WATERMELON *TSUKEMONO*

The watermelon white rind portion has a taste similar to cucumber.

Watermelon rind with a bit of red/yellow pulp
Salt
Green *shiso* leaves, *myoga*, lemon juice for extra flavor

Peel green rind off of watermelon pieces. Trim inside portion, retaining a little bit of red/yellow pulp. Cut rind into bite-size slices.

Place slices in a dish. Sprinkle lightly with salt. Refrigerate for 30 minutes. Less salt is better than too much salt at this stage. Drain salted slices. Taste and if not salty enough add more salt.

Serve with shreds of green *shiso* leaves as an edible garnish; thinly sliced *myoga* also adds zip. Lemon juice is a good additional seasoning.

OKRA AND ONION PICKLES (Okra *Shoyu-zuke*)

Eat okra raw? Try this—it's very good.

5–6 thumb-size okra, thinly sliced on diagonal
½ onion, thinly sliced (can be yellow or red/purple onion)
2 tablespoons rice vinegar
2 tablespoons *shoyu*

Place okra and onions in a container. Blend vinegar and *shoyu*. Mix well with okra and onions. Should be ready to serve in 1 hour.

As an accompaniment to *sake*, garnish with bonito flakes.

SLICED TURNIP PICKLES (*Kabu Kiri-zuke*)

2 bunches baby turnips with tops
2 teaspoons salt
Yuzu or lemon peel, thinly shredded
Lemon juice

Slice turnip bulbs into thin slices. Pour boiling water over green tops to blanch slightly. Mince into small pieces. Rub turnip and tops with salt. Put a ½ lb. (230 g) weight on top for 4–5 hours.

Serve in a small bowl with a garnish of *yuzu* or lemon peel. Add a bit of lemon juice on top.

ONION *TSUKEMONO*

Raw onions are quite harsh, but this is a most satisfactory method to flavor them. This will go well with any kind of meal.

1 large bulb onion, cut in half and
  sliced thinly
3½ tablespoons rice vinegar
1¾ tablespoons sugar
½ teaspoon salt
½ lemon, sliced and cut into small
  even pieces

Blanch onion quickly in boiling water. Drain well to remove excess water. Mix together vinegar, sugar, salt and lemon slices. Add to onion slices. Mix well. Allow to stand half a day. A tiny sprinkle of minced green parsley will make the serving very attractive.

Variation: Use red/purple onions.

FRIED CHINESE SPINACH
(*Kong-xin-cai Itame-zuke*)

Kong-xin-cai is a spinach-like vegetable. One can substitute spinach or swiss chard.

1 bunch *kong-xin-cai*
Several slices fresh ginger root
1 tablespoon sesame oil
2–3 teaspoons *shoyu*
Pinenuts, crushed walnuts or peanuts, optional

Wash a bunch of *kong-xin-cai*. Cut off hard stalk portions and coarsely chop. Fry ginger slices with sesame oil. Add *kong-xin-cai* and continue to fry briefly to wilt. Pour *shoyu* around edges. Serve in a dish with pinenuts or other nuts as garnish.

FRIED LEEK PICKLES
(*Jiu-huang-hua/Hoshi-ebi Itame-zuke*)

An intriguing combination using pickled leek that goes with many foods.

1 bunch leek stalks, cut into 1 inch (2.5 cm)
   lengths; remove hard portions
½ teaspoon salt
3 tablespoons dried shrimp
1 tablespoon sesame oil
Salt/pepper or *shoyu* as desired

Carefully wash leek stalks since sand/dirt collect at base. Salt leek stalks about 1 hour before starting to make this pickle. Rub leek lengths with salt. Put in a container and weight down. Let stand until liquid comes out.
   Toast dried shrimp in an ungreased frying pan until crisp. Crush shrimp with your hands. Return crushed shrimp to frying pan and add sesame oil. Add salted leek, washed and squeezed. Fry quickly. Season with salt or *shoyu*. Pepper can be sprinkled on top, if desired.

SALTED *BOK CHOY*
(*Bok Choy Shio-zuke*)

The Chinese have many vegetables suited for pickling and many varieties are now sold in America. Baby *bok choy* is very bland and not too strong in flavor.

1 lb. (450 g) baby *bok choy*
Salt—3% of weight of vegetable
Strips of dried *konbu* and red chili
   peppers (optional)

Wash baby *bok choy* well. Divide each head into half or quarters depending upon size of *bok choy*. Cut from base toward leaves with a knife, but stop about ⅓ from top. Tear rest of *bok choy* by hand, so leaves do not get sliced from knife blade.
   Sprinkle a little salt on bottom of a table top pickle-maker. Place baby *bok choy* in layers, sprinkling more salt. Repeat, alternating base and leaf end as you layer. A few strips of *konbu* and/or red chili peppers may be added for flavor.
   Screw weight on the pickle-maker for 2 hours. Release pressure. Turn *bok choy* upside down to evenly salt and weight down again. Should be ready in half a day.

Note: A good substitute for baby *bok choy* is Italian rabe or galucci. An interesting California-style variation is to add a few raisins or prunes into pickling jar with this type of salted *tsukemono*. A very subtle sweet taste results.
   The Chinese use pickled vegetables in cooking also. One favorite is *chung choi* (preserved turnip) which is added to soups, stir-fry dishes, etc. Sold in vacuum sealed plastic bags.

Fried Chinese Spinach

Fried Leek Pickles

Salted *Bok Choy*

73

CHRYSANTHEMUM FLOWERS (*Kiku*)

A seasonal taste that delights the older generations especially. The flower novelty enhances the charm of this special recipe. These edible *kiku* flowers are sold in the fall season in Asian markets. They can be used for an attractive garnish but, pickled, the flowers share their beauty on our menus.

SALTED CHRYSANTHEMUMS
(*Kiku Shio-zuke*)

3½ tablespoons salt
1½ tablespoons rice vinegar
½ lb. (230 g) edible *kiku* flowers

Wash flowers. Drain. Sprinkle a little salt on bottom of a pickling container and pack flowers in layers alternating with salt. Pour vinegar over and place a weight on top.

Liquid will come up overnight. Transfer flowers from pickling container to another jar and keep in refrigerator.

To prepare for serving, wash flowers under running water and then soak in water for 2 hours to remove harshness and salt. Squeeze water from flowers. Mix with boiled greens or salads. The photo shows boiled greens and *kiku* flowers dressed with a mixture of *shoyu* and some mustard powder.

INSTANT PICKLE MIXED WITH CHRYSANTHEMUMS

Cabbage, edible chrysanthemums and *shimeji* (small oyster mushrooms) combined together. *Kiku* flowers are called *"omoino hoka"* meaning unexpected. They are surprisingly delicious.

3 large cabbage leaves
1½ teaspoons salt
½ package fresh yellow *kiku* flowers
2 tablespoons rice vinegar
4 oz. (120 g) *shimeji* clusters
½ teaspoon salt
Sesame seeds (toasted), lemon juice and *shoyu*

Cut large cabbage leaves into strips. Coat with 1½ teaspoons salt. Place a 4 lb. (2 kg) weight on top. Pick petals from yellow *kiku* flowers. Blanch petals in boiling water with vinegar added. Rinse in cold water. Drain. Soak in vinegared water sufficient to cover.

Divide small *shimeji* into smaller clusters. Blanch in boiling water. Squeeze water from petals and *shimeji*. Add to cabbage. Sprinkle ½ teaspoon salt. Place weight over all. Before serving squeeze mixture firmly. Sprinkle crushed sesame seeds, lemon juice and *shoyu* on top.

CHRYSANTHEMUMS WITH MUSTARD
(*Kiku Karashi-zuke*)

Edible flowers can add spark to a meal.

1 package yellow *kiku* flowers
2 tablespoons rice vinegar
Dry mustard

Pick petals from yellow *kiku* flowers. Blanch petals briefly in boiling water with vinegar added. Scoop up petals with a skimmer. While petals are hot place in a container. Sprinkle dry mustard powder over little by little. Press petals down with a weight and after ½ day serve with a little *shoyu* sprinkled on top.

TURNIPS

Don't discard turnip tops! Turnip greens make an excellent pickle. To remove harshness from greens, sprinkle salt on them and squeeze after they become limp.

VINEGARED CHRYSANTHEMUMS AND TURNIPS
(*Kiku/Kabu Su-zuke*)

An example of Japanese artistic use of a vegetable and a flower.

1 lb. (500 g) turnips, peeled and cut lengthwise, then into half round shape
10 edible purple (or other color) *kiku* flowers
Mix together:
   1 tablespoon rice vinegar

1 tablespoon sugar
1 tablespoon salt

Place turnip and flower petals, which have been washed in water and squeezed, into a container. Pour vinegar, sugar and salt mixture on top. Place a light weight on top (such as two saucers). Liquid will ooze out overnight. Ready to serve.

TURNIPS AND TOPS PICKLED (*Kabu Tsukemono*)

This recipe uses both the tops and root of the vegetable.

2 bunches baby turnips with green tops
1 tablespoon grated *yuzu* (citron) or
    lemon peel
1 tablespoon salt
1 tablespoon sugar
1 red chili pepper, cut into rings
2 inch (5 cm) square dried *konbu*
2½ tablespoons rice vinegar

Cut off turnip tops. Put aside. Trim turnips if surface is stained. Cut into thin slices.

Mix salt and sugar together. Place part of this salt/sugar mixture barely covering bottom of a pickling container. Pack turnip slices compactly. Sprinkle remaining mixture with a little grated *yuzu* or lemon peel, red chili pepper rings and *konbu* on top. Pour rice vinegar over all.

To prepare greens: Use 1 teaspoon salt for about ½ lb. (230 g) of turnip tops. Sprinkle salt on greens and knead on a cutting board. Cut greens into 2 inch (5 cm) lengths. Put greens in a thick zip lock plastic bag. Remove air from bag. Put bag on top of sliced turnips, keeping stalks flat in bag. Put a 2 lb. (1 kg) weight on top of container. This *tsukemono* should be ready in 1 day.

Serve as arranged in photo.

DAIKON RADISH

The taste of *daikon* varies delightfully, depending on whether it is fresh, partially dried, or fully dried.

LEMON-FLAVORED *DAIKON* RADISH AND KIWI

The *daikon* and carrot will retain their crispness, with the soft kiwi as a complementary texture.

1 large *daikon*
1 medium carrot
½ teaspoon salt
2 kiwis
Pickling solution:
    1 tablespoon rice vinegar
    1 tablespoon lemon juice
    ¼ teaspoon salt

Cut peeled *daikon* and carrot into 1 inch (2.5 cm) long thin strips. Sprinkle salt over all. Once wilted, wash and squeeze water out.

Cut peeled kiwis in slices and then into thin strips.

Mix all in a bowl. Sprinkle pickling liquid over surface. Let stand 20 minutes and serve.

DAIKON COMBINATION (*Daikon Momi-zuke*)

Quick and easy to prepare at dinner hour.

½ *daikon* with leaves
½ carrot
¼ cup *kiri konbu* (*konbu* cut in strips)
1 teaspoon salt

Cut peeled *daikon* and carrot into thin strips. Blanch a small amount of soft inner *daikon* leaves in boiling water for a brief moment. Rinse in cold water. Squeeze water from leaves and mince.

Sprinkle salt on *daikon*, carrot, *kiri konbu* and minced *daikon* leaves. Rub well and squeeze liquid from vegetables firmly. Make just the amount needed for one mealtime serving.

SWEET VINEGARED DRIED *DAIKON*

(*Kiriboshi Daikon/Wakame Amazu-zuke*)

Two Japanese ingredients to experiment with. Crunchy texture.

4 oz. (120 g) shredded *daikon*, dried
2–3 strands of dried *wakame* seaweed
1 inch (2.5 cm) piece ginger root, peeled and cut
    into thin shreds

Soak dried *daikon* in warm water for 30 minutes to soften. Wash in water and squeeze firmly. Cut *wakame*, softened in water, into small pieces.

Pickling solution:
    ⅓ cup rice vinegar
    ⅓ teaspoon salt
    ⅓ teaspoon *shoyu*
    ½ tablespoon sugar

Mix pickling solution. Put *daikon*, *wakame* and ginger in a clean jar. Pour in pickling liquid. Mix lightly. Put a lid on container. Let stand 3–4 days.

WAKAME AND VEGETABLES *TSUKEMONO*

The combination of root crops and seaweed provides a delicious instant *tsukemono*. Very flavorful and plain, yet stimulating to your appetite.

3 cups *daikon*, sliced into 2 inch (5 cm) julienne
    strips
1 cup carrot, sliced into 2 inch (5 cm) julienne
    strips
5–6 strands of dried *wakame* seaweed
Salt
Pickling solution:
    3 tablespoons rice vinegar
    3 tablespoons sugar
    MSG (optional)

Pour boiling water over *wakame* pieces to soften. Do not soak too long. Drain well. Cut into bite-size pieces. Mix *daikon*, carrot and *wakame* together. Sprinkle a little salt and rub together. Pour a mixture of rice vinegar, sugar and MSG into vegetable mixture. Toss. Ready to serve.

CHINESE CABBAGE (*Hakusai*)

Chinese cabbage can be used either fresh or dried for half a day. Both leaves and stalk make good pickles.

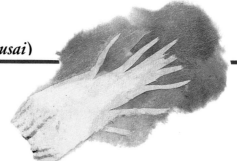

CHINESE CABBAGE PICKLED WITH KELP
(*Hakusai Konbu-zuke*)

Best if you can obtain a special type of *konbu* called *shio-konbu*, which has been boiled down in *shoyu* and covered with salt. The flavor of *shio-konbu* enhances the light taste of the cabbage. If not available, use *kiri konbu* and a sprinkle of salt. This *tsukemono* goes well with rice or bread.

1 lb. (450 g) Chinese cabbage
A few green soybeans in shell (use frozen ones if fresh not available)
1 oz. (30 g) *shio-konbu*
1 tablespoon rice vinegar
¼ teaspoon salt

Boil a lot of water in a large pan. Blanch cabbage leaves, base part first. Once base is wilted, soak rest of leaves in hot water briefly. To prevent excessive boiling, do not put all leaves in at one time but do two by two and keep water boiling uniformly. Squeeze water from cabbage. Cut *shio-konbu* into thin slices.

Coat green soybean shells with salt. Boil in boiling water briefly and cool in a colander. Remove beans from shells. Place cabbage and soybeans in a bowl. Add *shio-konbu*, vinegar and a little salt. Mix well. Put 2 plates or similar weight on top for about 1–2 hours until cabbage is seasoned lightly.

NUTRITIOUS CHINESE CABBAGE *TSUKEMONO*
(*Hakusai-zuke*)

An interesting blend of flavors as well as being most attractive.

2 heads Chinese cabbage
Salt equal to 4% of weight of cabbage
Handful *konbu* strips
½ dried cuttlefish (dried *surume*)—optional
Equal parts *mirin* and *shoyu* to cover
½ carrot, thinly sliced
½ onion, thinly sliced
1 *seri* (a type of parsley), chopped—optional
1 lemon or *yuzu* peel (if available), slivered into strips
2 red chili peppers, seeds removed, cut into rings

Pickle cabbage with salt for 3 days. Follow the general *shio-zuke* method, page 18. In meantime, soak *konbu* and cuttlefish in equal parts of *mirin* and *shoyu* to cover. In 24 hours, flavor of *konbu* and cuttlefish soaks into marinade. Then add the following: Carrot, onion, *seri*, lemon and chili pepper rings.

Drain cabbage and put *konbu*, cuttlefish and vegetable mixture between cabbage leaves. Place in a container and put a weight on top. Ready to serve in 3 days. Slice crosswise into 1 inch (2.5 cm) widths. Very pretty as well as healthy.

RAINBOW VEGETABLES (*Hakusai Chigusa-zuke*)

A delicate combination of vegetables lightly salted.

4 large Chinese cabbage leaves
2 inch (5 cm) length carrot
1 Japanese cucumber
1 inch (2.5 cm) piece fresh ginger root
5 radishes
Heaping teaspoon salt

Separate cabbage leaves into hard rib portions and soft leaves. Cut midribs lengthwise into 2 inch (5 cm) long thin strips. Cut leaves into large pieces from one end to the other.

Cut carrot, cucumber and ginger into 2 inch (5 cm) long shreds. Sprinkle salt over everything. Place a light weight over top. Let stand 15 minutes. Slice radishes into thin slivers and add

to above. Mix. Squeeze vegetables gently. Serve in a bowl so the glorious colors are evenly distributed on surface.

LEMON-FLAVORED CHINESE CABBAGE AND CLOUD EAR
(*Hakusai to Kikurage* Lemon-*zuke*)

Crunchy, unusual, tasty and easy to prepare

1–2 large dehydrated *kikurage* (wood ear, black fungus) or ½ cup fresh, if available
¾ lb. (330 g) Chinese cabbage
¾ inch (1.8 cm) piece fresh ginger, cut into thin strips
½ lemon, sliced into quarter-round thin sheer slices
1¼ to 1½ teaspoons salt

Reconstitute dried *kikurage* in lots of water. It will expand 5–6 times original size. Drain and pour boiling water on softened *kikurage*. Drain. Cut into approximately ¾ inch (1.8 cm) square pieces.

Separate hard midribs and soft leaves of Chinese cabbage. Cut midribs into 2 inch (5 cm) long thin slices. Cut leaves into larger bite-size pieces.

Mix all ingredients in a bowl. Put in a table top *tsukemono* jar. Screw down press. Juices will begin to ooze out quickly. Ready to serve in 30–45 minutes. This is an instant type pickle and not for long storage, although it will keep covered a day or so in refrigerator.

Note: If using fresh *kikurage* do not soak in water.

FIVE-COLOR PICKLES
(*Goshiki-zuke*)

Salted *shiso* seeds yield a burst of surprise flavor.

½ *daikon* radish
½ carrot
1 Japanese cucumber
1 celery rib with leaves
1½ teaspoons *sake*

Lemon-Flavored Chinese Cabbage and Cloud Ear

Curry-Flavored Cauliflower

Soy-Flavored *Daikon* Pickle

(Continued on page 84)

Five-Color Pickles

Cauliflower with
Pickle Sauce

Citron-Flavored *Daikon*

83

2 pinches salted *shiso* seeds, rinsed
(use amount you desire)
1 teaspoon salt

Cut *daikon* and carrot into thin strips. Cut cucumber into thin slices. Cut celery with strings removed into thin slices. Sprinkle *sake* on rinsed salted *shiso* seeds. Boil celery leaves for a brief moment. Cut into small pieces crosswise. Add salt and place a weight over all. Once liquid has oozed out, wash vegetables and squeeze dry. Ready to serve.

CURRY-FLAVORED CAULIFLOWER

Unusual spices give this pickle a distinctive flavor.

1 lb. (450 g) cauliflower, cut into florets
½ teaspoon salt
¼ lb. (120 g) *shimeji* oyster mushrooms)

Sprinkle salt on cauliflower florets. Cut base off of *shimeji* and discard. Split petite *shimeji* into small clusters. Blanch briefly. Mix with cauliflower.

Pickling solution:
  ½ cup rice vinegar
  3 tablespoons sugar
  ½ teaspoon salt
  dash cinnamon and cloves
  bay leaf
  ½ teaspoon curry powder

Combine all pickling solution ingredients except curry powder and bring to a boil. Cool. Then add curry powder. Soak cauliflower and *shimeji* in this cooled mixture for 1 day. Ready to serve.

CAULIFLOWER WITH PICKLE SAUCE
(Cauliflower *Itame-zuke*)

Try broccoflower (a green cauliflower/broccoli cross) in place of white cauliflower.

¾ lb. (330 g) cauliflower, separated into florets
1 Japanese cucumber, cut into 1½ inch (4 cm) long julienne strips
1 small carrot, cut crosswise in thin slices
1 tablespoon vegetable oil
1 teaspoon *sansho* powder
Dried chili pepper, seeded, cut into rings
Pickling solution:
  2 tablespoons sugar
  2 tablespoons rice vinegar
  1 teaspoon *shoyu*
  ¾ teaspoon salt

Blanch cauliflower in boiling water, drain and cool. Heat oil in frying pan. Fry red chili pepper rings, cauliflower, cucumber and carrot over high heat briefly. Add powdered *sansho* and mix. Remove vegetables. Set aside. Cook down pickling liquid until syrupy. Pour over vegetables. Ready to serve.

SOY-FLAVORED *DAIKON* PICKLE
(*Daikon Shoyu-zuke*)

¾ lb. (330 g) peeled *daikon* radish
¼ of a whole citron or lemon peel
2 tablespoons *shoyu*
½ tablespoon *sake*

Quarter *daikon* lengthwise. Cut each quarter crosswise into ⅓ inch (8 mm) thick slices. Make fine cuts on the surface.

Cut citron or lemon peel into fine shreds. Soak vegetables in a mixture of the *shoyu* and *sake*. Allow to stand, mixing occasionally. Ready to eat within one day.

CITRON-FLAVORED *DAIKON*

(*Daikon Yuko-zuke*)

²/₃ lb. (300 g) *daikon*, cut in half and then sliced
½ teaspoon salt

Sprinkle salt on *daikon* until wilted. Wash and drain.

Pickling solution:
   1 tablespoon rice vinegar
   1 tablespoon sugar
   ¼ teaspoon salt

½ *yuzu* citron or lemon, thinly sliced
1 red chili pepper, thinly shredded

Mixed all in a bowl. Sprinkle solution over surface. Put light weight on *daikon* for 2 hours.

DAIKON RADISH CHINESE STYLE

The flavor of *daikon* dried in the shade is different from the taste of fresh *daikon*.

1 lb. (450 g) *daikon*
Pickling solution:
   1½ tablespoons *shoyu*
   ½ teaspoon sesame oil or salad oil
   ½ teaspoon sugar
   sprinkling of red chili pepper

Cut *daikon* into thick ½ × ¼ inch (1.3 × 0.6 cm) strips. Spread out on a flat basket surface and dry in the shade for 2–3 hours. This will eventually become about ½ lb. (230 g).
   Marinate *daikon* with pickling mixture for 8 hours. Ready to serve.

Note: To speed process, fresh *daikon* can be sliced thinner.

ZUCCHINI WITH MUSTARD PICKLES

(Zucchini *Karashi-zuke*)

Suitable with rice or bread and another use for zucchini.

2 medium-size zucchini, unpeeled, cut into
   2 × ¼ inch (5 cm × 0.6 cm) slices.
3 tablespoons *shoyu*
1 teaspoon dry mustard powder
5–6 radish slices

Sprinkle 2 tablespoons *shoyu* on zucchini slices. This will reduce any bitterness and in 1 hour liquid will ooze out. Squeeze firmly. Coat zucchini with mixture of mustard and 1 tablespoon *shoyu*. Add radish slices. Place a light weight on top. Ready to serve in 30 minutes.

Quick *Tsukemono*

Peppery Cucumber

Lemon Turnip

Pickled *Daikon*
Radish with Spice

PICKLED *DAIKON* RADISH WITH SPICE

(*Daikon Yakumi-zuke*)

4-inch (10 cm) long piece *daikon* radish, cut
   crosswise into ¼ inch (0.6 cm) slices
Daikon leaves, minced (optional)
1 small carrot, shredded fine
1 knob fresh ginger root, shredded fine
1 stalk green onion or scallions, minced
1 teaspoon salt
1 teaspoon toasted white sesame seeds, crushed
   with fingers to release fragrance
A few drops sesame oil

Mix *daikon* slices, *daikon* leaves, carrot shreds,
ginger shreds and green onion with salt. Place in
a table-top pickling container. Weight down. Let
stand 30 minutes. Discard liquid. Squeeze lightly.
Sprinkle sesame seeds. Add a few drops of
sesame oil just before serving, since it enhances
pickle.

Pickled Green Pepper
with Seaweed Tea

Asparagus with
Bean Paste

ASPARAGUS WITH BEAN PASTE

(Asparagus *Miso-zuke*)

Fresh asparagus means spring has come. Try this
with a simple marinade.

1 lb. (450 g) green asparagus
1 cup *miso*
Mirin
2 pieces cheesecloth

Break off hard portions of asparagus stalks. Peel
skin if too tough. Blanch in salted boiling water
briefly. Place in cold water to cool off. Drain.
Dilute *miso* with *mirin* to form a soft paste. Place
half of *miso* paste at bottom of a bowl. Put piece
of cheesecloth over mixture. Then place aspara-

Spicy Cabbage
Tsukemono

gus, cheesecloth and another layer of *miso* paste.

Ready in 2–3 hours. Prepare only enough for one meal. Too long in pickling base hardens asparagus.

Note: This same recipe base can be used for other similar textured vegetables such as okra, kohlrabi, etc.

SPICY CABBAGE *TSUKEMONO*
(Cabbage *Shoyu-zuke*)

Slightly cooked cabbage flavored with chili pepper, oil and soy sauce.

6–8 large cabbage leaves
4 tablespoons salad oil
5 tablespoons *shoyu*
1 red chili pepper with seeds removed

Cut cabbage leaves into small pieces from one end to the other. Put in a bowl. Pour boiling water over leaves and turn over once. Discard water immediately. Stir leaves to cool slightly.

Heat frying pan with oil. Add small slices of red chili pepper and stir. Remove from heat. Mix *shoyu* with red chili pepper oil and pour mixture on cabbage leaves which have cooled down slightly by now. Mix. Let stand 30 minutes. Ready to serve.

PICKLED GREEN PEPPER WITH SEAWEED TEA
(*Piman Kobucha-zuke*)

An interesting way of using powdered seaweed tea (*kobucha*), which comes in a small can.

1 teaspoon commercially sold *kobucha*
½ cup boiled water which has been cooled
Dash salt

4 Japanese green peppers or 2 Western green peppers*

Place *kobucha*, water and salt in a pickling container. Add halved green peppers and weight down. Ready to serve in 3–4 hours. Green pepper absorbs flavor of the *konbu* in the powdered tea.

* **Note:** If using Western type green pepper cut into slices lengthwise.

LEMON TURNIP
(*Kabu* Lemon-*zuke*)

The tang of lemon goes well with turnips.

1 bunch baby turnips
1 lemon
Salt equal to 1½–2% weight of turnips

Cut off tops from turnips, leaving ½ inch (1.3 cm) stems. Wash dirt out of stalks thoroughly. Cut turnips lengthwise into thin slices. In case of bigger turnips, cut in half first.

Mix thinly sliced lemon with turnips. Sprinkle salt lightly over turnips. Put in pickling container and place weight over all. Ready in 2–3 hours.

PEPPERY CUCUMBER
(*Kyuri Togarashi Miso-zuke*)

2 cucumbers
1 tablespoon *tou-ban-jang*
   (Chinese hot bean paste)
MSG (optional)

Rub cucumber with salt. Wipe off and slice into bite-sized pieces.

Mix *tou-ban-jang* and MSG in a bowl. Add cucumbers. Place in pickling container. Place light weight (one plate) on top. Let stand one hour. Add 1 teaspoon *shoyu*, if desired.

Part III
Pacific Rim
Pickles...
and
More

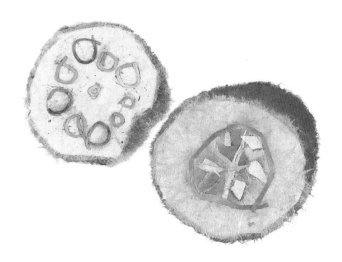

HOT PEPPER PICKLES
(Chinese)

A tantalizing flavor, different from Japanese-style *tsukemono* but equally good with meals.

4 cups Chinese cabbage, white rib sections only, finely shredded, 2-inches (5 cm) long
2 teaspoons salt
2 tablespoons salad oil
3 dried small red chili peppers
Pickling solution:
   1½ tablespoons sugar
   1 tablespoon rice vinegar

Add salt to shredded Chinese cabbage in a large container. Mix. Weight down Chinese cabbage with a few saucers. Let soak and ferment 4–8 hours in kitchen at room temperature. Drain off water and do not squeeze. Heat pickling solution to dissolve sugar. Put aside.

   Heat oil over medium heat for ½ minute and add dried chili peppers. Stir-fry a few minutes until almost black. Remove pan from stove and pour hot oil into pickling solution. It will sizzle and spurt. Pour mixture over salted cabbage and mix well. Can be served right away or be kept in refrigerator for up to 2–3 weeks.

Note: Cucumbers, sliced thinly, can be substituted. Experiment with other vegetables of your choice.

RADISH PICKLES
(Chinese)

Crushed, crisp radishes, flavored mildly, can be served instantly.

25 fresh radishes, washed
¼ teaspoon salt
Pickling solution:
   1 tablespoon *shoyu*
   1½ tablespoons rice vinegar
   1 teaspoon sugar
   1 teaspoon sesame oil
   ¼ teaspoon salt

Trim radishes, leaving some green leaves at top. Chill in ice water for about 15 minutes. Drain. Whack crisp radishes with bottom of a glass. This will crack them. Sprinkle ¼ teaspoon salt. Return to refrigerator to chill another 15 minutes.

   Combine all pickling ingredients and pour over drained radishes just before the meal. Mix well.

SHANGHAI DELIGHT
(Chinese)

This is a fine accompaniment for noodles and dumplings as well as for rice. Kohlrabi and chayote squash are good substitutes for *daikon*.

1 medium-size *daikon* radish or
   1 lb. (450 g) turnips
1 teaspoon salt
2 teaspoons sugar
2 tablespoons *shoyu*
2 teaspoons (or less) sesame oil

Clean and wash *daikon*. Not necessary to peel if quite whitish and very fresh. Dry well with a clean cloth. Cut into small cubes. Put *daikon*, salt and sugar into a large sterilized jar.

Cover. Shake jar well. Refrigerate overnight. Discard liquid. Pour in *shoyu*. Shake jar again and soak 2 hours. Garnish with sesame oil just before serving. Keeps in refrigerator for 2–3 weeks.

ACHARA (Filipino)

1 large green papaya (about 4 cups when peeled
   and seeds removed)
Pickling solution:
   ¼ cup cider vinegar
   ½ teaspoon salt
   1 teaspoon sugar
   1 red chili pepper, minced
   1 tablespoon ginger root, grated

Prepare papaya and cut into very fine shreds. Mix all ingredients together. Pack in a clean container and refrigerate overnight.

Note: Green papayas are increasingly available in American markets due to the influx of Southeast Asian refugees to the West Coast. Green papaya flesh is nearly white and similar in color to *daikon*.

KIM CHEE (Korean)

Kim chee is a highly seasoned pickle of Korea. It can be made with cabbage, Chinese cabbage, cucumbers, *daikon*, turnips and other vegetables. To enhance and vary the flavor, dried shrimp, fish or shellfish can be added. The smell is very pungent but one can very easily become addicted! One taste leads to another.

1 head Chinese cabbage (3 lbs.; 1.5 kg), cut 2 inch (5 cm) lengths
¼ cup rock salt
1 cup water
1 tablespoon sugar
1 teaspoon salt
1 knob ginger root, minced fine
3 stalks green onions, sliced thin diagonally (including green tops)
1–3 cloves garlic (or use more), crushed
3 teaspoons (or use less) ground red pepper

Slice cabbage, put in large bowl. Add ¼ cup rock salt and water. Mix well and keep at room temperature about 10 hours. Drain and rinse. Squeeze out excess water and put cabbage in a large bowl.

Mix all ingredients together with cabbage. Taste a small piece of cabbage and adjust seasonings for salt, etc. Pack in sterilized jar, pressing down firmly. Cover. Leave at warm room temperature 1 or 2 days. (One day for summer and two days for winter.) Put in refrigerator to store. Ready to eat.

SOUR BEAN SPROUTS (Vietnamese)

½ lb. (250 g) fresh bean sprouts
1 green onion, sliced into 5 pieces (use green tops)
1 small piece ginger root, sliced like matchsticks (optional)
1 cup water
1 tablespoon white vinegar
2½ tablespoons sugar
½ teaspoon salt

If time permits, trim roots from bean sprouts. Wash and drain. Put bean sprouts, green onions and ginger in a bowl. Set aside.

Boil water, vinegar, sugar and salt to dissolve. Cool to room temperature. Pour over vegetables in bowl. Stir to mix well.

After 30 minutes mix again. Ready in about 1–2 hours. Drain before serving. Or leave at room temperature all day to ferment. Refrigerate. Keeps 4 days.

CARROT/*DAIKON* RELISH (Vietnamese)

Very delicate and can be used with any cosmopolitan meal, but especially suitable for certain barbecued meats Vietnamese-style.

1 5-inch (13 cm) length carrot
1 5-inch (13 cm) length *daikon* radish
1 cup water
2 teaspoons cider vinegar
2 teaspoons sugar
Pinch salt
Cilantro

Cut 3 "V" shaped lengthwise wedges into carrot and *daikon* surfaces so when thinly sliced crosswise, flower shapes will result.

  Mix all ingredients and marinate for at least 1 hour. Drain. Serve along with meat dishes. Garnish with cilantro.

GREEN PAPAYA PICKLES (Thai)

Green papaya pulp is similar to white *daikon* but tart and crunchy. Not sweet like the yellow ripe papaya from the tropics.

1 large green papaya, peeled and seeded
  or substitute (½ lb.; 250 g) carrot or cucumber
1 clove garlic
2 red chili peppers, seeded (use discretion)
½ cup cherry tomatoes, halved (or 1 tomato, sliced)
2 tablespoons minced onions
1 teaspoon minced green onions (use green tops)
Juice of 1 lime (2–3 tablespoons)
1 teaspoon fish sauce (*nam pla*)
1 teaspoon sugar

Garnishes: 2 inch (5 cm) square chunks cabbage, loose butter lettuce leaves, wedges fresh lime, cilantro, mint or even long string beans. Ground peanuts and salted shrimp make this authentically Thai. Slices of red/green chili peppers would also enhance the pickle.

  Shred papaya using a mandolin-type grater. If carrot or cucumber is substituted, slice in long thin strips. Grind garlic and chili peppers. Mix with all other ingredients and toss lightly. This can be kept briefly in refrigerator to chill.

  Eat along with cabbage or lettuce and other edible garnishes.

MAUI-STYLE PICKLED ONIONS (Hawaiian)

Mild flavored pickles that go with any meal. If available, try Vidalia onions. They are so sweet tasting that you can eat them like an apple.

Select small to medium-size onions, enough to
fill a quart jar, after cutting in half or quarters.
Pickling solution:
  1 clove garlic, peeled
  2 chili peppers, seeds removed
  cider vinegar
  water
  1 tablespoon pickling salt
  1 teaspoon sugar

Fill a quart jar with onion halves/quarters. Put in garlic and chili peppers. Fill with vinegar ⅔ full. Fill with water the remaining ⅓ space in jar. Add salt and sugar. Cover. Shake thoroughly. Allow to stand 2–3 days, but shake once each day. Refrigerate for a few days for full flavor penetration.

HAWAIIAN-STYLE *TAKUAN*

This *takuan* is often called Hawaiian-style although it has been commonly made in the States for generations. This is the type sold in jars in supermarkets. Flavor is different from *nukazuke takuan* but yet slightly similar.

Fresh *daikon*, about 6–7 large long *daikon* will fill
4 quarts (4.5 *l*)
  Dry *daikon* in sun for 3–4 days until limp. Wash, slice into ½ inch (1 cm) rounds or 2 inch (5 cm) long sticks. Pack in sterilized jars.
Pickling solution:
  4 cups water
  4 cups sugar
  2 cups cider vinegar
  ½ cup salt

Boil water, add sugar and vinegar. Boil together and cool. Add salt and cook another 2 minutes more. Use while hot. Pour syrup over *daikon* and seal immediately. Let jars stand for 2–3 weeks or until *daikon* turns a light yellow color. Keeps in refrigerator up to 1½ months. Strong aroma, so keep well covered.

Two red chili peppers may be added to each quart jar while packing. This solution is enough for about 4 quarts of *daikon*.

Note: This recipe can be adjusted as one would adjust other pickles—more salt, less sugar, etc.

ARMENIAN PICKLES

This special pickle was developed in the Fresno, California area by a Japanese-American friend. It goes especially well with all Asian type foods as well as with any Western-style buffet. Easy and keeps well.

Pickling solution:
6 cups water
3 cups white distilled vinegar
1 cup sugar
⅓ cup salt

Put above ingredients in a stainless steel or enamel pot. Bring to boil. Cool. In a gallon jar, place 2 or 3 cloves garlic and 1 or more crushed dried red chili peppers. Pack jar with vegetables of your choice cut into large chunks, slices or florets. Push vegetables down into jar so they will not float up later.

Suggested vegetables:
    asparagus
    cabbage
    cauliflower
    celery
    carrots
    turnips
    cucumbers
    bell peppers
    green beans
    green tomatoes
    broccoli

Fill jar with brine and add another clove of garlic and 1 whole crushed chili pepper on top. Leave out 24 hours to ferment, then refrigerate. Make it on Tuesday, refrigerate on Wednesday and serve it on Saturday. It will last about a month in the refrigerator although it will get stronger . . . but still be very tasty.

PICKLED SQUID

(*Ika Tsukemono*)

Squid prepared in an entirely different manner from the Western concept.

1 lb. (450 g) squid, cleaned, remove innards and beak
2 cups water
Marinade:
    2 tablespoons *shoyu*
    2 tablespoons rice vinegar
    ¼ cup *sake* or sherry
    1 tablespoon sugar

Wash cleaned squid and cut into ¼ inch (6 mm) slices. Heat water to boiling and add squid. Stir for 2 minutes over medium heat until cooked. Do not overcook. Drain and discard liquid or save for stock.

Cook marinade over medium heat. Simmer about 4 minutes until slightly thickened. Pour hot over cooked squid. Mix. Place in refrigerator for 3 hours or overnight to chill. This will keep for one day.

GINGER/SARDINE *TSUKUDANI*

An unusual combination to add to your cornucopia of pickling ideas.

1 lb. (450 g) fresh ginger root
3⅓ oz. (100 g) dried tiny sardines (*chirimen-jako*)
1½ cups *sake*
5 tablespoons or more sugar
½ cup *mirin*
½ cup *shoyu*

Select firm ginger roots and wash well. Shred into matchstick lengths. Soak in water and drain. Spread out to dry for 3–4 hours.

Place ginger shreds and tiny sardines in a saucepan. Add *sake*. Heat. After boiling point is reached, stir and add sugar, *mirin* and *shoyu*. Stir and simmer until most of liquid has evaporated. Do not scorch. Cool and place in a clean jar in refrigerator.

LEFTOVER *NORI*

6 sheets toasted *nori*, torn into tiny pieces
1 dried *shiitake* mushroom soaked in water, squeezed and chopped into tiny pieces
2½ tablespoons *shoyu*
3½ tablespoons *mirin*
Several pinches powdered mix for *dashi* soup stock
5 tablespoons water
¼ tablespoon sugar (optional)

Put *nori* in heavy pan with *shiitake*. Mix *shoyu*, *mirin*, *dashi* and water. Stir to dissolve. Combine with *nori* and *shiitake*. Stir well. Cook over medium heat to boiling stage. Reduce heat and cook about 10 minutes. Keep stirring so it will not scorch. This yields about ¾ cup and keeps in refrigerator several weeks. As additional flavoring, *shiso* or ginger can be added.

FISH MARINATED WITH *SAKE* LEES
(*Sakana Kasu-zuke*)

This delicious grilled fish will certainly make you a devotee for life! This version is quite salty, but not as much as the traditional method.

3 lbs. (1.3 kg) salmon or butterfish (sablefish) fillets with skin, if possible
2 tablespoons salt
1 cup *sake* lees (*kasu*)
½ cup sugar
½ cup *sake*

Cut salmon in serving size pieces. Place in a bowl. Salt both sides and allow to stand in refrigerator covered for 1–2 days. Fish will become firm. Drain liquid. Do not wash off salt but pat dry. Mix *sake* lees (*kasu*), sugar and *sake*. Cover fish pieces well with mixture. Keep refrigerated. Ready to use in about 2–3 days. Leave a thin layer of *kasu* mixture on fish. Broil until *kasu* has caramelized and fish flakes at edges. Be careful not to burn. Serve small portions with hot rice.

COOKED AND PICKLED KELP
(*Nori Tsukudani*)

Some of the very ambitious West Coast folks have been harvesting *nori* (*porphyra* variety) along the Pacific coastal shores for years. They lug buckets and sacks filled with the sandy, dark purplish-brown hued marine vegetable home. It is washed ever so carefully to remove sand particles and then dried. Uses are many—for soups, pickles, etc. Here is how to prepare your harvest in the *tsukudani* manner.

½ lb. (250 g) dried *wakame* or hand-harvested *nori*, dried
1 cup water
1 teaspoon vinegar
6 tablespoons *shoyu*
4 tablespoons sugar
2 tablespoons *sake*

Soak *wakame* or *nori* in cold water to reconstitute seaweed. This will also remove additional sand particles, if any. Rinse, drain. Chop into smallish pieces. Put *wakame* or *nori* in pan. Add water and vinegar. Cook over low heat until softened and add *shoyu*, sugar and *sake*. Simmer over low heat again until most of the liquid has evaporated. Stir occasionally so it will not scorch.

KELP *FURIKAKE*

This pulverized condiment is delicious with hot rice, or sprinkle a dash on top of soup.

3½ oz. (105 g) kelp
⅔ oz. (20 g) dried bonito flakes
1 sheet *nori*, toasted
1 tablespoon white sesame seeds, toasted
Dash red pepper flakes
Dash salt

Clean kelp with a clean cloth. Chop up into small pieces. Quickly toast dried bonito flakes (watch so they will not burn). Place kelp in food processor to pulverize. Add bonito flakes and *nori*. Briefly turn on. Place in a small mixing bowl. Add toasted sesame seeds, red pepper flakes and salt.

Note: An interesting addition to this combination is to add a sprinkling of *yukari* (pulverized salted red *shiso* leaves) page 27.

MUSHROOMS WITH CARROTS

Not a *tsukemono*, but delicious as a condiment to have with rice.

5 large dried *shiitake* mushrooms, soaked in
    water 30 minutes, squeezed dry
1 carrot
4 tablespoons *dashi* stock
2 tablespoons *shoyu*
1 tablespoon *mirin*
1 tablespoon sugar
Oil for frying
Red chili pepper flakes

Shred *shiitake* in fine strips. Cut carrot in shreds to match *shiitake*. Heat oil and stir-fry *shiitake* and carrot over low heat. Add *dashi* stock, *shoyu*, *mirin* and sugar. When flavor has penetrated, add red chili pepper flakes. Stir to mix well. Keep in refrigerator.

Note: Burdock (*gobo*) can be added, cut in fine strips.

SOY SAUCE PICKLED VEGETABLES
(*San-bai-zuke*)

A pickle with good flavors mingled together.

5 cups *daikon*
4 cups cucumber
1 cup carrot
2 cups eggplant
¼ cup salt
1½ cups *shoyu*
2 cups sugar
3 tablespoons rice vinegar
MSG (optional)
1–2 chili peppers
1 knob ginger root, grated

Cut *daikon*, cucumber, carrot and eggplant in thin slices and soak overnight in salt. Rinse with cold water. Squeeze hard. This will remove any bitterness in vegetables.

Boil *shoyu*, sugar, vinegar and MSG (optional) and when it begins to boil add vegetables including chili peppers and ginger. Mix well and drain vegetables. Save liquid. Boil this liquid again for 2 minutes. Add vegetables and mix. Pour into a sterilized jar and refrigerate.

LOTUS ROOT PICKLES (*Su-basu*)

Lotus roots are khaki-colored bulbs (a rhizome) connected in a chain of 2–3 sections. The inside core of each bulb has openings lengthwise, and when sliced crosswise the open "canals" in the root appear lacy. Crunchy lotus root can be used for pickles, stir-frying, soups, salads and even deep-fried like potato chips.

1 lb. (450 g) fresh lotus root
1 tablespoon rice vinegar
1½ cups water
Pickling solution:
   ½ cup rice vinegar
   ¼ cup sugar
   ½ cup water
   Dash salt
   1 dried red chili pepper

Mix 1 tablespoon rice vinegar and 1½ cups water. Simmer over low heat. Peel lotus root and cut into thin slices. Drop slices into the hot acidulated water mixture. Cook 5 minutes. Drain and cool. Place in a clean jar. Prepare pickling mixture except for the red chili pepper. Bring to boil. Pour hot syrup over cooked lotus roots. Sprinkle sliced red chili pepper, seeded, over top. Cover. Best flavor develops after a few days. This will keep well in the refrigerator. Ideal for garnishing *sushi*, broiled seafood or to nibble as a pickle.

BREAD *TSUKEMONO* BASE

This can be substituted for *nuka-doko*. (See page 31).

1 lb. (450 g) bread, any kind except sweet
3 cups water
4 tablespoons pickling salt

Tear bread into pieces. Add water and knead. Mix in salt. Continue to knead until pasty. Let stand half a day and it will be ready to use. Soak vegetables in this bread paste. Flatten surface of paste. Keep refrigerated. Pickling time is the same as with the *nuka-doko* method.

Commercially prepared instant *nukamiso-zuke* mixes are sold for the busy housewife to use as a pickling base.

BEER *TSUKEMONO* BASE

Try this beer base for pickles with a difference. Easy to make and ingredients are easy to obtain.

2 cans beer
½ cup salt
2 cups brown sugar
1 small box oatmeal (about 5 cups)
Fresh vegetables (cucumbers, broccoli, celery, eggplant, Chinese cabbage, *etc.*)

Mix all ingredients together well. Add freshly washed vegetables. Keep this pickling bowl in refrigerator. Cucumbers and Chinese cabbage will be ready in 1 day. Other denser vegetables will take an extra day or more. Rinse before serving. As liquid rises in the bed, drain off. Every time new vegetables are added sprinkle in some more salt. This is important. In this manner pickling bed can last up to one year.

FRUIT LIQUEURS (*Kajitsu-shu*)

These are versatile and suit a festive occasion. The flavor is soft and mild, similar to the taste of a quality liqueur. Keeps for many years if stored properly in a cool, dark place.

ABCs of HOMEMADE *KAJITSU-SHU*

• Use fresh seasonal fruit. Choose fruit just before maturity, without bruises. Every fruit variety differs slightly. Over-ripe fruit does not hold its shape well and liqueur will be cloudy.

Wash fruit well and wipe water completely from surface one by one with a dry cloth. Water causes molding.

• The Japanese use white liquor (*shochu*) 35 proof, or substitute a good grade of vodka. White liquor is a clear and soft alcohol distilled from sweet potatoes, rice or millet. The higher the proof, the sooner liquor will extract fruit essence. Too high proof liquor will be too strong to drink.

• Crystal rock sugar (*zarame* or *kōrizato*) is a sugar of high purity which melts into a clear liquid. Its real taste does not overpower the natural sweetness of fruit. If not available substitute granulated sugar, however, it will make a somewhat cloudy and sweeter result.

• Keep *kajitsu-shu* in a sealed container in a cool, dark place. A wide-mouth glass mason jar with a tight fitting lid which can seal the jar completely is easiest to use. Sterilize jar and lid. See directions page 13.

Label jar with fruit and date of preparation. Store in a closet or other dry, cool, dark place with the least temperature change. Refrigerator is not appropriate for storage since temperature is too low for *kajitsu-shu* to ferment. Appropriate temperature for maturing is 59–68°F (15–20°C).

Plum Wine (*Ume-shu*)

Fruit Punch

Pineapple Liqueur

Plum Liqueur

Orange Liqueur

Pomegranate Liqueur

- Liqueurs are very sweet so serve accordingly.
  - ☆ Instead of little liqueur glasses, use a 6 oz. (240 g) glass which allows the bouquet and aroma of the liqueur to show itself.
  - ☆ Serve straight from the jar.
  - ☆ With ice cubes or diluted with water.
  - ☆ As a mixed drink blended with other fruit *kajitsu-shu* or juice.
  - ☆ Serve as a punch with soda water.
  - ☆ Use as an ingredient in cakes, in frostings, and in cooking.
  - ☆ The fruit used in *kajitsu-shu* is edible and delicious.
  - ☆ Eat it plain, prepare into a jam, or pour over ice cream.

PLUM WINE (*Ume-shu*)

This is the most popular *kajitsu-shu*, and it is simple to make.

2.2–3.3 lbs. (1~1.5 kg) green *ume* plums or try unripe apricots
3¾ pints (1.8 *l*) white liquor or vodka
1–1½ lbs. (450~500 g) crystal rock sugar

Remove stems from *ume* plums. Soak in cold water. Wash plums well and drain. Wipe water from surface one by one with a clean cloth. Prick 4–5 holes in each plum with a thick toothpick.

Put plums and crystal rock sugar in a sterilized jar, filling ⅘ of jar height. Pour white liquor to cover. Seal jar with a sterilized lid. Keep in a cool, dark place. In 3 months it should be ready. The longer the maturing period the better the taste. Serve chilled or over ice. Remove plums after 1 year.

Note: This basic preparation method can be used with other fruits.

FRUIT PUNCH

A harmonious blending of fruit flavors.

1½ cups orange *liqueur* (see next page for recipe)
1 cup pineapple *liqueur* (see next page for recipe)
1 cup soda water
Sugar to taste
Lemon slices, pineapple slices or cherries for garnish

Blend all above ingredients, adding sugar to taste. Refrigerate and serve with a garnish floating on top.

ORANGE LIQUEUR

Very refreshing sourness. Try early tart Valencia oranges for this recipe. (When fully ripe they are too sweet for liqueur making.)

2 medium-size tart oranges
2 pints (0.9 *l*) white liquor or vodka
5–7 oz. (150~210 g) crystal rock sugar

Pour boiling water on 1 orange to soften wax on the peel. Cool a little. Scrub wax off surface with a nylon brush. Repeat process with the other orange. Remove peel and pith (the white portions surrounding orange sections). Cut sections crosswise into ½ inch (1.2 cm) slices. Save cleaned peel of 1 orange. Put orange slices, rind of 1 orange (all white pith removed) and crystal rock sugar in a bottle. Pour in liquor. Remove peel after 1 week.

PINEAPPLE LIQUEUR

This has a very distinctive flavor.

½–1 fresh pineapple
2 pints (0.9 *l*) white liquor or vodka
5–7 oz. (150~210 g) crystal rock sugar

Cut leaves off of pineapple and wash surface. Shave off peel with a knife. Cut pineapple lengthwise in half, and then cut into wedges. Remove center hard core portion (about ¾ inch /1.8 cm width). Cut peel into ½ inch (1.2 cm) slices. Put pineapple wedges, core and peel in a sterilized jar. Add liquor and crystal rock sugar. Remove fruit and peel in 2–3 months when it has matured.

PLUM LIQUEUR

Beautiful jewel color and mild taste.

1 lb. (450 g) Santa Rosa plums, not quite fully ripened
2 pints (0.9 *l*) white liquor or vodka
7–9 oz. (210~270 g) crystal rock sugar

Wash plums well. Wipe off water with a clean cloth one by one. Make pricks on each plum surface. Put plums, crystal rock sugar and white liquor in a sterilized jar. Leave plums in jar. After a year they can be removed. Keep in a dark, cool place. Maturing period is 3 months or more.

POMEGRANATE LIQUEUR

Sweet taste with soft exquisite color. Make this *kajitsu-shu* around October when pomegranates are ripe.

3–4 large pomegranates
2 pints (0.9 *l*) white liquor or vodka
5–7 oz. (150~210 g) crystal rock sugar

Put pomegranate seed kernels, white liquor and crystal rock sugar in a sterilized jar. In 6–7 months, remove pomegranates. Serve this *kajitsu-shu* with lemon slices.

MARINATED FRUIT/*RUMTOPF*

The best *rumtopf* combinations use many fruits and have a good thick, rich syrup which improves in flavor as the months pass.

Melon balls
Fresh or canned pineapple chunks
Whole strawberries
Fresh peaches, peeled and sliced, or frozen or canned peaches
Granulated sugar
Light rum, white liquor or vodka (60 proof)

Optional fruit suggestions:
    Cherries, apricots, pears, raspberries, plums or grapes

Layer about 1 inch (2.5 cm) of each fruit in a large crock. Sprinkle each layer with equal amount of sugar. Add rum or other liquor to cover fruit ½ inch (1.2 cm).

Cover with plastic wrap so alcohol will not evaporate (optional). Put cover on crock. Leave at room temperature 70°F (21°C). Often people keep a crock "going" on the kitchen counter. Allow at least a month for the flavors to intermingle. *Rumtopf* will keep maturing.

Any firm fruit may be used. New fruit may be added as mature fruit is removed. Add more sugar and liquor. At serving time, serve *rumtopf* from the crock. Very tasty plain or spooned like a sauce over ice cream, cake squares or pudding.

SUGARED APRICOTS (*Anzu Sato-zuke*)

A delightful way to prepare apricots. Adding some pickled red *shiso* leaves gives a special delectable touch. This recipe is from the Nagano area of Japan.

8.8 lbs. (4 kg) firm ripe apricots
7/8 cup salt
8½ cups sugar
1 cup rice vinegar
2 cups white liquor or vodka
Pickled red *shiso* leaves (optional) from *umeboshi*

Cut apricots in half. Save seeds. Put all into a clean jar. Sprinkle salt on them. Place a drop lid or saucer over apricots for 24 hours. Wash and drain in a colander. Wipe off water and dry completely with a clean cloth. Place apricots and seeds in a jar. Mix 1¼ cups sugar, half of the vinegar and half of the white liquor. Allow to marinate for 24 hours. Transfer to a colander to drain.

Separate seeds from this batch of apricots. Place seeds in a hole punched heavy plastic bag, nylon net or cheesecloth bag. Put apricots and remaining sugar, vinegar and white liquor in a bowl. Mix well. Adding some red *shiso* leaves pickled in *umeboshi* at this stage is optional but a surprisingly desirable flavor results.

Return entire contents of bowl into jar. Place bag with seeds as a weight on top in place of a lid. Put a saucer with a light weight over the bag. Allow juices just to cover the apricots. Keep in a cool, dark place until matured in 2 months. Serve as a savory tid-bit with tea.

KUMQUAT PRESERVES

Firm, miniature orange-type citrus fruit. Oval or round shape, about 1-inch in diameter and 1~1½-inch (2~3.5 cm) long. To eat fresh, squeeze whole fruit between fingers to stimulate oils in the skin. Pop entire unpeeled fruit in your mouth and while chewing, tart juices from the pulp will intermingle with the sweet skin. The flavor is most unexpected and one can become very addicted.

Preserved, the fruit is excellent with all kinds of meals or as a snack. It is especially treasured in Japan and China. The fruit in Japanese is called *kinkan*—golden orange.

1 lb. (450 g) kumquats
Cold water for initial cooking process
1½ teaspoons *sake*
1 cup sugar
1¼ cups water

Wash kumquats well. Remove any stems. Rinse several times. Drain. Place kumquats in a sauce-pan, cover with cold water and add *sake*. Bring to the boiling point and reduce heat to simmer fruit for 10 minutes. Drain. Fruit will be soft. After cooling, use a needle or toothpick to prick the skin surface in 4 or 5 places. (Some people cut a small cross at the base.) This prevents the fruit from bursting during the preserving process and at the same time allows fruit to absorb the syrup.

Combine 1¼ cups water with the sugar. Boil over low heat, stirring constantly to dissolve sugar. Simmer syrup for 3 minutes. Put blanched kumquats in pan with hot syrup and simmer about 25 minutes until fruit is transparent. Remove pot from heat and allow fruit to plump up overnight in the syrup. Reheat syrup with kumquats to the boiling point and pack in a sterilized jar. Seal. Or place in a covered jar in refrigerator. Keeps well.

Variation: 4 sheer slices of lemon added to kumquats about 10 minutes before cooking is completed will enhance and add a distinctive flavor.

CRYSTALIZED GINGER

A sweet tid-bit loved by Americans. A specialty chocolate candy shop dips them into semi-sweet dark chocolate. Myriad of uses for cakes, cookies, ice cream, chutneys, glazes and meat/fish sauces. Use tender young fiber-free ginger root. Fresh ivory-colored and rosy-tipped roots are available January/February and July/August.

⅔ lb. (300 g) ginger root
Dash cider vinegar
2½ cups granulated sugar
1½ cups water
Granulated sugar for sprinkling

Scrape off ginger root peel and thinly slice. Soak in water with a dash of vinegar to remove spiciness for 1 hour. Rinse and drain. Put 2½ cups sugar and water in a heavy saucepan. Heat until dissolved. Add ginger slices. Stir occasionally until liquid is like honey. Do not stir too much or the syrup will not form properly. Turn off heat. Spread out on a rack to cool, exposing ginger to air. Sprinkle with granulated sugar before it has cooled completely. Store in an air-tight container.

GLOSSARY

age (*abura-age*)—deep fried soybean cake (*tofu*).

an—sweetened red *azuki* beans prepared as a paste for confections.

amazake—non-alcoholic creamy-thick hot drink prepared from rice fermented with addition of rice *koji*.

anzu—apricot.

bok choy—very mild vegetable of Chinese origin, member of chard family. White ribs with dark green leaves. Baby (petite) size stalks now available.

bonito—a type of tuna.

chayote—a member of the squash family, pale green exterior with ridged surface and a large seed inside.

chili peppers—use tiny Japanese dried red peppers sold in small packets.

chirimen-jako—dried tiny sardines.

daikon—long white Japanese radish, twelve inches (30 cm) or more in length.

dashi—Japanese seaweed stock prepared from kelp and dried bonito.

drop lid—a necessary item for Japanese pickling. A wooden cover which is smaller in circumference than pot opening, so lid will lay flat on top of food, and weight can be placed on top of lid.

dou-ban-jiang—spicy Chinese brown bean paste, contains chili.

fish sauce—*nuoc mam* (Vietnamese); *nam pla* (Thai); prepared from preserved fish or shrimp and salt.

ginger—use fresh ginger root (rhizomes). Do not substitute dried ground ginger powder.

hakusai—Chinese cabbage; celery cabbage.

hanagiri daikon—sun-dried *daikon* radish.

itame—to fry.

jicama—a vegetable of Mexican origin, similar to a giant turnip.

jiu-huang-hua—a flowering Chinese scallion.

kabu—round turnips.

kabocha—a Japanese squash.

kajitsu-shu—fruit liqueurs.

karashi—Japanese mustard.

kasu—*sake* lees.

katsuobushi—dried bonito flakes.

kelp—edible seaweed.

kikurage—cloud or wood ear mushroom, edible black fungus (dried).

kiku—chrysanthemum.

kinkan—kumquat.

kiriboshi daikon—sun-dried *daikon* radish cut into thin strips.

kiri-konbu—dried kelp cut into thin strips.

koji—a yeast-like rice mold that works primarily to convert starches into sugars during a fermentation process.

konbu—kelp.

kobucha—tea made from dried, powdered kelp.

korizato—crystal rock sugar.

konnyaku—jellied devil's tongue an edible tubor.

kong-xin-cai—a spinach-like Chinese vegetable.

kyona—a feathery, leafy green vegetable similar to mustard greens.

mirin—a thick sweet wine made from glutinous rice, used primarily for cooking.

miso—fermented soybean paste.

mizuna—a feathery, leafy green vegetable similar to mustard greens. Called *kyona* in Kyoto area.

mochiko—glutinous rice flour.

mochi—glutinous rice that has been pounded until soft and sticky, then formed into cakes.

mochigome—glutinous rice.

mochi-gashi—a confection made from glutinous rice.

myoga—young, pinkish fresh ginger shoots.

nanohana—yellow flower of the rape plant.

nasu or *nasubi*—Japanese eggplant, usually less than half the size of American eggplant.

natto—fermented soybeans with sticky texture and strong aroma.

nori—edible seaweed, laver.

nuka—rice bran.

rice vinegar—made from glutinous rice, fragrant and mild.

sake or *shu*—a double-fermented rice "wine."

sake **lees**—the residue from making *sake*, called in Japanese *kasu* or *sake-gasu*.

sakura—cherry.

sashimi—sliced raw fish.

sansho—a fragrant condiment made from dried, ground prickly ash berries.

sato—sugar.

shimeji—*Pleurotus ostreatus*; a greyish-white mushroom that grows with overlapping oyster shell-shaped caps. Ideal flavor when immature and caps are tiny.

shio—salt.

shiratamako—refined glutinous rice flour.

shiro uri—a melon of the gourd family; looks like a long, fat, white cucumber.

shiso—*Perilla frutescens*; plant related to the mint family, with aromatic leaves. Both red- and green-leaf varieties are available, and each tastes different.

shiitake—a large, dark-brown mushroom used both fresh and dried. This flavorful mushroom is used often in Japanese cooking.

shochu—white liquor made from sweet potatoes, rice or grains.

shoyu—Japanese soy sauce, considerably lighter than Chinese soy sauce, which should not be substituted for *shoyu*.

su—rice vinegar.

suribachi—Japanese pestle and mortar (earthenware bowl with ridged sides)

takana—a variety of mustard green.

takuan—pickled yellow *daikon* radish.

togarashi—chili pepper.

toko—pickling bed.

tsukemono—Japanese pickled foods, primarily vegetables.

tsukudani—food simmered with *shoyu*, sugar, *mirin* and water until almost all liquid evaporates.

ume—Japanese plum; technically a species of apricot, but usually translated as plum.

umeboshi—pickled plum.

uri—see *shiro uri*.

wakame—an edible seaweed, thinner and softer than *konbu* kelp.

wasabi—Japanese green horseradish, most familiar in the West as a mound of pungent green paste served with *sushi* and *sashimi*.

white liquor—*shochu*.

yuzu—lemon-like citrus fruit.

zarame—crystal rock sugar.

Note: In Japanese when an adjective is combined with a noun, sometimes there is a slight change in phonetics. Some examples:

* *sake* becomes *zake*
* *sushi* becomes *zushi*
* *sato* becomes *zato*
* *tsuke* (soak) becomes *zuke*
* *toko* (pickling bed) becomes *doko*

INDEX